The Birthday Party
and
The Room

THE BIRTHDAY PARTY
and
THE ROOM

Two plays by Harold Pinter

GROVE PRESS, INC.   NEW YORK

The Birthday Party copyright © 1959
by Harold Pinter
The Room copyright © 1960 by Harold Pinter

These plays are fully protected by copyright. All inquiries concerning performing rights, professional or amateur, readings or any other use of this material should be directed to the author's sole agents: ACTAC (Theatrical and Cinematic) Ltd. 16 Cadogan Lane, London, S. W. 1

Printed in the United States of America

Contents

The Birthday Party *page* 7

The Room *page* 91

To Vivien

The Birthday Party

THE BIRTHDAY PARTY was first presented by Michael Codron and David Hall at the Arts Theatre, Cambridge, on 28 April, 1958, and subsequently at the Lyric Opera House, Hammersmith, with the following cast:

PETEY, *a man in his sixties*	Willoughby Gray
MEG, *a woman in her sixties*	Beatrix Lehmann
STANLEY, *a man in his late thirties*	Richard Pearson
LULU, *a girl in her twenties*	Wendy Hutchinson
GOLDBERG, *a man in his fifties*	John Slater
MC CANN, *a man of thirty*	John Stratton

Directed by Peter Wood

ACT I   A morning in summer

ACT II   Evening of the same day

ACT III   The next morning

Act One

The living-room of a house in a seaside town. A door leading to the hall down left. Back door and small window up left. Kitchen hatch, centre back. Kitchen door up right. Table and chairs, centre.

PETEY *enters from the door on the left with a paper and sits at the table. He begins to read.* MEG'S *voice comes through the kitchen hatch.*

MEG. Is that you, Petey?

Pause.

Petey, is that you?

Pause.

Petey?
PETEY. What?
MEG. Is that you?
PETEY. Yes, it's me.
MEG. What? (*Her face appears at the hatch*). Are you back?
PETEY. Yes.
MEG. I've got your cornflakes ready. (*She disappears and reappears.*) Here's your cornflakes.

He rises and takes the plate from her, sits at the table, props up the paper and begins to eat. MEG *enters by the kitchen door.*

Are they nice?
PETEY. Very nice.
MEG. I thought they'd be nice. (*She sits at the table.*) You got your paper?
PETEY. Yes.

MEG. Is it good?
PETEY. Not bad.
MEG. What does it say?
PETEY. Nothing much.
MEG. You read me out some nice bits yesterday.
PETEY. Yes, well, I haven't finished this one yet.
MEG. Will you tell me when you come to something good?
PETEY. Yes.

Pause.

MEG. Have you been working hard this morning?
PETEY. No. Just stacked a few of the old chairs. Cleaned up a bit.
MEG. Is it nice out?
PETEY. Very nice.

Pause.

MEG. Is Stanley up yet?
PETEY. I don't know. Is he?
MEG. I don't know. I haven't seen him down yet.
PETEY. Well then, he can't be up.
MEG. Haven't you seen him down?
PETEY. I've only just come in.
MEG. He must be still asleep.

> *She looks round the room, stands, goes to the sideboard and takes a pair of socks from a drawer, collects wool and a needle and goes back to the table.*

What time did you go out this morning, Petey?
PETEY. Same time as usual.
MEG. Was it dark?
PETEY. No, it was light.
MEG (*beginning to darn*). But sometimes you go out in the morning and it's dark.
PETEY. That's in the winter.
MEG. Oh, in winter.
PETEY. Yes, it gets light later in winter.

MEG. Oh.

Pause.

What are you reading?
PETEY. Someone's just had a baby.
MEG. Oh, they haven't! Who?
PETEY. Some girl.
MEG. Who, Petey, who?
PETEY. I don't think you'd know her.
MEG. What's her name?
PETEY. Lady Mary Splatt.
MEG. I don't know her.
PETEY. No.
MEG. What is it?
PETEY (*studying the paper*). Er—a girl.
MEG. Not a boy?
PETEY. No.
MEG. Oh, what a shame. I'd be sorry. I'd much rather have a little boy.
PETEY. A little girl's all right.
MEG. I'd much rather have a little boy.

Pause . . . Vaguely.

Is it nice out?
PETEY. Yes, it's a nice day.
MEG. Is the sun shining?
PETEY. Yes.
MEG. I wish Stanley would take me for a walk along the front one day. When was I last along the front? Why don't you ask him to take me for a walk one day, Petey?
PETEY. Why don't you ask him yourself?
MEG. No. You ask him.

Pause.

He goes through his socks terrible.
PETEY. Why? He's in bed half the week.

MEG. That boy should be up. Why isn't he up? What's the time?
PETEY. About half past ten.
MEG. He should be down. He's late for his breakfast.
PETEY. I've finished my cornflakes.
MEG. Were they nice?
PETEY. Very nice.
MEG. I've got something else for you.
PETEY. Good.

She rises, takes his plate and exits into the kitchen. She then appears at the hatch with two pieces of fried bread on a plate.

MEG. Here you are, Petey.

He rises, collects the plate, looks at it, sits at the table. MEG re-enters.

Is it nice?
PETEY. I haven't tasted it yet.
MEG. I bet you don't know what it is.
PETEY. Yes, I do.
MEG. What is it, then?
PETEY. Fried bread.
MEG. That's right.

He begins to eat.

PETEY. No bacon?
MEG. I've run out.
PETEY. Ah.
MEG. I'm going out soon, to do some shopping.

She watches him eat.

PETEY. Very nice.
MEG. I knew it was.
PETEY (*turning to her*). Oh, Meg, two men came up to me on the beach last night.
MEG. Two men?

PETEY. Yes. They wanted to know if we could put them up for a couple of nights.
MEG. Put them up? Here?
PETEY. Yes.
MEG. How many men?
PETEY. Two.
MEG. What did you say?
PETEY. Well, I said I didn't know. So they said they'd come round to find out.
MEG. Are they coming?
PETEY. Well, they said they would.
MEG. Had they heard about us, Petey?
PETEY. They must have done.
MEG. Yes, they must have done. They must have heard this was a very good boarding house. It is. This house is on the list.
PETEY. It is.
MEG. I know it is.
PETEY. They might turn up today. Can you do it?
MEG. Oh, I've got that lovely room they can have.
PETEY. You've got a room ready?
MEG. I've got the room with the armchair all ready for visitors.
PETEY. You're sure?
MEG. Yes, that'll be all right then, if they come today.
PETEY. Good.

She takes the socks etc. back to the sideboard drawer.

MEG. I'm going to wake that boy.
PETEY. There's a new show coming to the Palace.
MEG. On the pier?
PETEY. No. The Palace, in the town.
MEG. Stanley could have been in it, if it was on the pier.
PETEY. This is a straight show.
MEG. What do you mean?
PETEY. No dancing or singing.
MEG. What do they do then?

PETEY. They just talk.

   Pause.

MEG. Oh.
PETEY. You like a song, eh, Meg?
MEG. I like listening to the piano. I used to like watching Stanley play the piano. Of course, he didn't sing. (*Looking at the door.*) I'm going to call that boy.
PETEY. Didn't you take him up his cup of tea?
MEG. I always take him up his cup of tea. But that was a long time ago.
PETEY. Did he drink it?
MEG. I made him. I stood there till he did. I tried to get him up then. But he wouldn't, the little monkey. I'm going to call him. (*She goes to the door.*) Stan! Stanny! (*She listens.*) Stan! I'm coming up to fetch you if you don't come down! I'm coming up! I'm going to count three! One! Two! Three! I'm coming to get you! (*She exits and goes upstairs. In a moment, shouts from* STANLEY, *wild laughter from* MEG. PETEY *takes his plate to the hatch. Shouts. Laughter.* PETEY *sits at the table. Silence. She returns.*) He's coming down. (*She is panting and arranges her hair.*) I told him if he didn't hurry up he'd get no breakfast.
PETEY. That did it, eh?
MEG. I'll get his cornflakes.

   MEG *exits to the kitchen.* PETEY *reads the paper.* STANLEY *enters. He is unshaven, in his pyjama jacket and wears glasses. He sits at the table.*

PETEY. Morning, Stanley.
STANLEY. Morning.

   Silence. MEG *enters with the bowl of cornflakes, which she sets on the table.*

MEG. So he's come down at last, has he? He's come down at

ACT I] THE BIRTHDAY PARTY 15

last for his breakfast. But he doesn't deserve any, does he, Petey? (STANLEY *stares at the cornflakes.*) Did you sleep well?

STANLEY. I didn't sleep at all.

MEG. You didn't sleep at all? Did you hear that, Petey? Too tired to eat your breakfast, I suppose? Now you eat up those cornflakes like a good boy. Go on.

He begins to eat.

STANLEY. What's it like out today?
PETEY. Very nice.
STANLEY. Warm?
PETEY. Well, there's a good breeze blowing.
STANLEY. Cold?
PETEY. No, no, I wouldn't say it was cold.
MEG. What are the cornflakes like, Stan?
STANLEY. Horrible.
MEG. Those flakes? Those lovely flakes? You're a liar, a little liar. They're refreshing. It says so. For people when they get up late.
STANLEY. The milk's off.
MEG. It's not. Petey ate his, didn't you, Petey?
PETEY. That's right.
MEG. There you are then.
STANLEY. All right, I'll go on to the second course.
MEG. He hasn't finished the first course and he wants to go on to the second course!
STANLEY. I feel like something cooked.
MEG. Well, I'm not going to give it to you.
PETEY. Give it to him.
MEG (*sitting at the table, right*). I'm not going to.

Pause.

STANLEY. No breakfast.

Pause.

All night long I've been dreaming about this breakfast.

MEG. I thought you said you didn't sleep.
STANLEY. Day-dreaming. All night long. And now she won't give me any. Not even a crust of bread on the table.

Pause.

Well, I can see I'll have to go down to one of those smart hotels on the front.
MEG (*rising quickly*). You won't get a better breakfast there than here.

She exits to the kitchen. STANLEY *yawns broadly.* MEG *appears at the hatch with a plate.*

Here you are. You'll like this.

PETEY *rises, collects the plate, brings it to the table, puts it in front of* STANLEY, *and sits.*

STANLEY. What's this?
PETEY. Fried bread.
MEG (*entering*). Well, I bet you don't know what it is.
STANLEY. Oh yes I do.
MEG. What?
STANLEY. Fried bread.
MEG. He knew.
STANLEY. What a wonderful surprise.
MEG. You didn't expect that, did you?
STANLEY. I bloody well didn't.
PETEY (*rising*). Well, I'm off.
MEG. You going back to work?
PETEY. Yes.
MEG. Your tea! You haven't had your tea!
PETEY. That's all right. No time now.
MEG. I've got it made inside.
PETEY. No, never mind. See you later. Ta-ta, Stan.
STANLEY. Ta-ta.

PETEY *exits, left.*

Tch, tch, tch, tch.

MEG (*defensively*). What do you mean?
STANLEY. You're a bad wife.
MEG. I'm not. Who said I am?
STANLEY. Not to make your husband a cup of tea. Terrible.
MEG. He knows I'm not a bad wife.
STANLEY. Giving him sour milk instead.
MEG. It wasn't sour.
STANLEY. Disgraceful.
MEG. You mind your own business, anyway. (STANLEY *eats*.) You won't find many better wives than me, I can tell you. I keep a very nice house and I keep it clean.
STANLEY. Whoo!
MEG. Yes! And this house is very well known, for a very good boarding house for visitors.
STANLEY. Visitors? Do you know how many visitors you've had since I've been here?
MEG. How many?
STANLEY. One.
MEG. Who?
STANLEY. Me! I'm your visitor.
MEG. You're a liar. This house is on the list.
STANLEY. I bet it is.
MEG. I know it is.

He pushes his plate away and picks up the paper.

Was it nice?
STANLEY. What?
MEG. The fried bread.
STANLEY. Succulent.
MEG. You shouldn't say that word.
STANLEY. What word?
MEG. That word you said.
STANLEY. What, succulent—?
MEG. Don't say it!
STANLEY. What's the matter with it?
MEG. You shouldn't say that word to a married woman.
STANLEY. Is that a fact?

MEG. Yes.
STANLEY. Well, I never knew that.
MEG. Well, it's true.
STANLEY. Who told you that?
MEG. Never you mind.
STANLEY. Well, if I can't say it to a married woman who can I say it to?
MEG. You're bad.
STANLEY. What about some tea?
MEG. Do you want some tea? (STANLEY *reads the paper.*) Say please.
STANLEY. Please.
MEG. Say sorry first.
STANLEY. Sorry first.
MEG. No. Just sorry.
STANLEY. Just sorry!
MEG. You deserve the strap.

>*She takes his plate and ruffles his hair as she passes.* STANLEY *exclaims and throws her arm away. She goes into the kitchen. He rubs his eyes under his glasses and picks up the paper. She enters.*

I brought the pot in.
STANLEY (*absently*). I don't know what I'd do without you.
MEG. You don't deserve it though.
STANLEY. Why not?
MEG (*pouring the tea, coyly*). Go on. Calling me that.
STANLEY. How long has that tea been in the pot?
MEG. It's good tea. Good strong tea.
STANLEY. This isn't tea. It's gravy!
MEG. It's not.
STANLEY. Get out of it. You succulent old washing bag.
MEG. I am not! And it isn't your place to tell me if I am!
STANLEY. And it isn't your place to come into a man's bedroom and—wake him up.
MEG. Stanny! Don't you like your cup of tea of a morning—the one I bring you?

ACT I] THE BIRTHDAY PARTY 19

STANLEY. I can't drink this muck. Didn't anyone ever tell you to warm the pot, at least?
MEG. My father wouldn't let you insult me the way you do.
STANLEY. Your father? Who was he when he was at home?
MEG. He would report you.
STANLEY (*sleepily*). Now would I insult you, Meg? Would I do a terrible thing like that?
MEG. You did.
STANLEY (*putting his head in his hands*). Oh God, I'm tired.

Silence. MEG *goes to the sideboard, collects a duster, and vaguely dusts the room, watching him. She comes to the table and dusts it.*

Not the bloody table!

Pause.

MEG. Stan?
STANLEY. What?
MEG (*shyly*). Am I really succulent?
STANLEY. Oh, you are. I'd rather have you than a cold in the nose any day.
MEG. You're just saying that.
STANLEY (*violently*). Look, why don't you get this place cleared up! It's a pigsty. And another thing, what about my room? It needs sweeping. It needs papering. I need a new room!
MEG (*sensual, stroking his arm*). Oh, Stan, that's a lovely room. I've had some lovely afternoons in that room.

He recoils from her hand in disgust, stands and exits quickly by the door on the left. She collects his cup and the teapot and takes them to the hatch shelf. The street door slams. STANLEY *returns.*

MEG. Is the sun shining? (*He crosses to the window, takes a cigarette and matches from his pyjama jacket, and lights his cigarette.*) What are you smoking, Stan?

STANLEY. A cigarette.
MEG. Are you going to give me one?
STANLEY. No.
MEG. I like cigarettes. (*He stands at the window, smoking. She crosses behind him and tickles the back of his neck.*) Tickle, tickle.
STANLEY (*pushing her*). Get away from me.
MEG. Are you going out?
STANLEY. Not with you.
MEG. But I'm going shopping in a minute.
STANLEY. Go.
MEG. You'll be lonely, all by yourself.
STANLEY. Will I?
MEG. Without your old Meg. I've got to get things in for the two gentlemen.

A pause. STANLEY *slowly raises his head. He speaks without turning.*

STANLEY. What two gentlemen?
MEG. I'm expecting visitors.

He turns.

STANLEY. What?
MEG. You didn't know that, did you?
STANLEY. What are you talking about?
MEG. Two gentlemen asked Petey if they could come and stay for a couple of nights. I'm expecting them. (*She picks up the duster and begins to wipe the cloth on the table.*)
STANLEY. I don't believe it.
MEG. It's true.
STANLEY (*moving to her*). You're saying it on purpose.
MEG. Petey told me this morning.
STANLEY (*grinding his cigarette*). When was this? When did he see them?
MEG. Last night.
STANLEY. Who are they?

MEG. I don't know.
STANLEY. Didn't he tell you their names?
MEG. No.
STANLEY (*pacing the room*). Here? They wanted to come here?
MEG. Yes, they did. (*She takes the curlers out of her hair.*)
STANLEY. Why?
MEG. This house is on the list.
STANLEY. But who are they? I mean, why. . . . ?
MEG. You'll see when they come.
STANLEY (*decisively*). They won't come.
MEG. Why not?
STANLEY (*quickly*). I tell you they won't come. Why didn't they come last night, if they were coming?
MEG. Perhaps they couldn't find the place in the dark. It's not easy to find in the dark.
STANLEY. They won't come. Someone's taking the Michael. Forget all about it. It's a false alarm. A false alarm. (*He sits at the table.*) Where's my tea?
MEG. I took it away. You didn't want it.
STANLEY. What do you mean, you took it away?
MEG. I took it away.
STANLEY. What did you take it away for?
MEG. You didn't want it!
STANLEY. Who said I didn't want it?
MEG. You did!
STANLEY. Who gave you the right to take away my tea?
MEG. You wouldn't drink it.

    STANLEY *stares at her.*

STANLEY (*quietly*). Who do you think you're talking to?
MEG (*uncertainly*). What?
STANLEY. Come here.
MEG. What do you mean?
STANLEY. Come over here.
MEG. No.
STANLEY. I want to ask you something. (MEG *fidgets nerv-*

ously. She does not go to him.) Come on. (*Pause.*) All right. I can ask it from here just as well. (*Deliberately.*) Tell me, Mrs. Boles, when you address yourself to me, do you ever ask yourself who exactly you are talking to? Eh?

Silence. He groans, his trunk falls forward, his head falls into his hands.

MEG (*in a small voice*). Didn't you enjoy your breakfast, Stan? (*She approaches the table.*) Stan? When are you going to play the piano again? (STANLEY *grunts.*) Like you used to? (STANLEY *grunts.*) I used to like watching you play the piano. When are you going to play it again?
STANLEY. I can't, can I?
MEG. Why not?
STANLEY. I haven't got a piano, have I?
MEG. No, I meant like when you were working. That piano.
STANLEY. Go and do your shopping.
MEG. But you wouldn't have to go away if you got a job, would you? You could play the piano on the pier.

He looks at her, then speaks airily.

STANLEY. I've . . . er . . . I've been offered a job, as a matter of fact.
MEG. What?
STANLEY. Yes. I'm considering a job at the moment.
MEG. You're not.
STANLEY. A good one, too. A night club. In Berlin.
MEG. Berlin?
STANLEY. Berlin. A night club. Playing the piano. A fabulous salary. And all found.
MEG. How long for?
STANLEY. We don't stay in Berlin. Then we go to Athens.
MEG. How long for?
STANLEY. Yes. Then we pay a flying visit to . . . er . . . whatsisname. . . .
MEG. Where?

STANLEY. Constantinople. Zagreb. Vladivostok. It's a round the world tour.

MEG (*sitting at the table*). Have you played the piano in those places before?

STANLEY. Played the piano? I've played the piano all over the world. All over the country. (*Pause.*) I once gave a concert.

MEG. A concert?

STANLEY (*reflectively*). Yes. It was a good one, too. They were all there that night. Every single one of them. It was a great success. Yes. A concert. At Lower Edmonton.

MEG. What did you wear?

STANLEY (*to himself*). I had a unique touch. Absolutely unique. They came up to me. They came up to me and said they were grateful. Champagne we had that night, the lot. (*Pause.*) My father nearly came down to hear me. Well, I dropped him a card anyway. But I don't think he could make it. No, I—I lost the address, that was it. (*Pause.*) Yes. Lower Edmonton. Then after that, you know what they did? They carved me up. Carved me up. It was all arranged, it was all worked out. My next concert. Somewhere else it was. In winter. I went down there to play. Then, when I got there, the hall was closed, the place was shuttered up, not even a caretaker. They'd locked it up. (*Takes off his glasses and wipes them on his pyjama jacket.*) A fast one. They pulled a fast one. I'd like to know who was responsible for that. (*Bitterly.*) All right, Jack, I can take a tip. They want me to crawl down on my bended knees. Well I can take a tip . . . any day of the week. (*He replaces his glasses, then looks at* MEG.) Look at her. You're just an old piece of rock cake, aren't you? (*He rises and leans across the table to her.*) That's what you are, aren't you?

MEG. Don't you go away again, Stan. You stay here. You'll be better off. You stay with your old Meg. (*He groans and lies across the table.*) Aren't you feeling well this morning, Stan? Did you pay a visit this morning?

He stiffens, then lifts himself slowly, turns to face her and speaks low and meaningfully.

STANLEY. Meg. Do you know what?
MEG. What?
STANLEY. Have you heard the latest?
MEG. No.
STANLEY. I'll bet you have.
MEG. I haven't.
STANLEY. Shall I tell you?
MEG. What latest?
STANLEY. You haven't heard it?
MEG. No.
STANLEY (*advancing*). They're coming today.
MEG. Who?
STANLEY. They're coming in a van.
MEG. Who?
STANLEY. And do you know what they've got in that van?
MEG. What?
STANLEY. They've got a wheelbarrow in that van.
MEG (*breathlessly*). They haven't.
STANLEY. Oh yes they have.
MEG. You're a liar.
STANLEY (*advancing upon her*). A big wheelbarrow. And when the van stops they wheel it out, and they wheel it up the garden path, and then they knock at the front door.
MEG. They don't.
STANLEY. They're looking for someone.
MEG. They're not.
STANLEY. They're looking for someone. A certain person.
MEG (*hoarsely*). No, they're not!
STANLEY. Shall I tell you who they're looking for?
MEG. No!
STANLEY. You don't want me to tell you?
MEG. You're a liar!

A sudden knock on the front door. MEG *edges past*

STANLEY *and collects her shopping bag. Another knock on the door.* MEG *goes out.* STANLEY *sidles to the door and listens.*

VOICE. Hullo Mrs. Boles. It's come.
MEG. Oh, has it come?
VOICE. Yes, it's just come.
MEG. What, is that it?
VOICE. Yes. I thought I'd bring it round.
MEG. Is it nice?
VOICE. Very nice. What shall I do with it?
MEG. Well, I don't . . . (*Whispers.*)
VOICE. No, of course not . . . (*Whispers.*)
MEG. All right, but . . . (*Whispers.*)
VOICE. I won't . . . (*Whispers.*) Ta-ta, Mrs. Boles.

STANLEY *quickly sits at the table. Enter* LULU.

LULU. Oh, hullo.
STANLEY. Ay-ay.
LULU. I just want to leave this in here.
STANLEY. Do. (LULU *crosses to the sideboard and puts a solid, round parcel upon it.*) That's a bulky object.
LULU. You're not to touch it.
STANLEY. Why would I want to touch it?
LULU. Well, you're not to, anyway.
STANLEY. Sit down a minute.

LULU *walks upstage.*

LULU. Why don't you open the door? It's all stuffy in here.

She opens the back door.

STANLEY (*rising*). What are you talking about? I disinfected the place this morning.
LULU (*at the door*). Oh, that's better.
STANLEY. Don't you believe me, then?
LULU. What?
STANLEY. Don't you believe I scrubbed the place out with Dettol this morning?

LULU. You didn't scrub yourself, I suppose?
STANLEY. I was in the sea at half past six.
LULU. Were you?
STANLEY. Sit down.
LULU. A minute.

She sits, takes out a compact and powders her nose.

STANLEY. So you're not going to tell me what's in that parcel?
LULU. Who said I knew?
STANLEY. Don't you?
LULU. I never said so.
STANLEY (*triumphantly*). Well, how can you tell me what's in it if you don't know what's in it?
LULU. I'm not going to tell you.
STANLEY. I think it's going to rain today, what do you think?
LULU. Why don't you have a shave?
STANLEY. Don't you believe me then, when I tell you I was in the sea at half past six this morning?
LULU. I'd rather not discuss it.
STANLEY. You think I'm a liar then?
LULU (*offering him the compact*). Do you want to have a look at your face? (STANLEY *withdraws from the table.*) You could do with a shave, do you know that? (STANLEY *sits, right, at the table.*) Don't you ever go out? (*He does not answer.*) I mean, what do you do, just sit around the house like this all day long? (*Pause.*) Hasn't Mrs. Boles got enough to do without having you under her feet all day long?
STANLEY. I always stand on the table when she sweeps the floor.
LULU. Why don't you ever go out?
STANLEY. I was out—this morning—before breakfast—
LULU. I've never seen you out, not once.
STANLEY. Well, perhaps you're never out when I'm out.
LULU. I'm always out.
STANLEY. We've just never met, that's all.

LULU. Why don't you have a wash? You look terrible.
STANLEY. A wash wouldn't make any difference.
LULU (*rising*). Come out and get a bit of air. You depress me, looking like that.
STANLEY. Air? Oh, I don't know about that.
LULU. It's lovely out. And I've got a few sandwiches.
STANLEY. What sort of sandwiches?
LULU. Cheese.
STANLEY. I'm a big eater, you know.
LULU. That's all right. I'm not hungry.
STANLEY (*abruptly*). How would you like to go away with me?
LULU. Where.
STANLEY. Nowhere. Still, we could go.
LULU. But where could we go?
STANLEY. Nowhere. There's nowhere to go. So we could just go. It wouldn't matter.
LULU. We might as well stay here.
STANLEY. No. It's no good here.
LULU. Well, where else is there?
STANLEY. Nowhere.
LULU. Well, that's a charming proposal. (*He gets up.*) Are you going to wash?
STANLEY (*going round to her*). Listen. I want to ask you something.
LULU. You've just asked me.
STANLEY. No. Listen. (*Urgently.*) Has Meg had many guests staying in this house, besides me, I mean before me?
LULU. Besides you?
STANLEY (*impatiently*). Was she very busy, in the old days?
LULU. Why should she be?
STANLEY. What do you mean? This used to be a boarding house, didn't it?
LULU. Did it?
STANLEY. Didn't it?
LULU. Did it?

STANLEY. Didn't . . . oh, skip it.
LULU. Why do you want to know?
STANLEY. She's expecting two guests, for the first time since I've been here.
LULU. Oh. Do you have to wear those glasses?
STANLEY. Yes.
LULU. So you're not coming out for a walk?
STANLEY. I can't at the moment.
LULU. You're a bit of a washout, aren't you?

> *She exits, left.* STANLEY *stands. He then goes to the mirror and looks in it. He goes into the kitchen, takes off his glasses and begins to wash his face. A pause. Enter, by the back door,* GOLDBERG *and* MCCANN. MCCANN *carries two suitcases,* GOLDBERG *a briefcase. They halt inside the door, then walk downstage.* STANLEY, *wiping his face, glimpses their backs through the hatch.* GOLDBERG *and* MCCANN *look round the room.* STANLEY *slips on his glasses, sidles through the kitchen door and out of the back door.*

MCCANN. Is this it?
GOLDBERG. This is it.
MCCANN. Are you sure?
GOLDBERG. Sure I'm sure.

> *Pause.*

MCCANN. What now?
GOLDBERG. Don't worry yourself, McCann. Take a seat.
MCCANN. What about you?
GOLDBERG. What about me?
MCCANN. Are you going to take a seat?
GOLDBERG. We'll both take a seat. (MCCANN *puts down the suitcases and sits at the table, left.*) Sit back, McCann. Relax. What's the matter with you? I bring you down for a few days to the seaside. Take a holiday. Do yourself a favour. Learn to relax, McCann, or you'll never get anywhere.

MCCANN. Ah sure, I do try, Nat.

GOLDBERG (*sitting at the table, right*). The secret is breathing. Take my tip. It's a well-known fact. Breathe in, breathe out, take a chance, let yourself go, what can you lose? Look at me. When I was an apprentice yet, McCann, every second Friday of the month my Uncle Barney used to take me to the seaside, regular as clockwork. Brighton, Canvey Island, Rottingdean—Uncle Barney wasn't particular. After lunch on Shabbuss we'd go and sit in a couple of deck chairs—you know, the ones with canopies —we'd have a little paddle, we'd watch the tide coming in, going out, the sun coming down—golden days, believe me, McCann. (*Reminiscent.*) Uncle Barney. Of course, he was an impeccable dresser. One of the old school. He had a house just outside Basingstoke at the time. Respected by the whole community. Culture? Don't talk to me about culture. He was an all-round man, what do you mean? He was a cosmopolitan.

MCCANN. Hey, Nat. . . .

GOLDBERG (*reflectively*). Yes. One of the old school.

MCCANN. Nat. How do we know this is the right house?

GOLDBERG. What?

MCCANN. How do we know this is the right house?

GOLDBERG. What makes you think it's the wrong house?

MCCANN. I didn't see a number on the gate.

GOLDBERG. I wasn't looking for a number.

MCCANN. No?

GOLDBERG (*settling in the armchair*). You know one thing Uncle Barney taught me? Uncle Barney taught me that the word of a gentleman is enough. That's why, when I had to go away on business I never carried any money. One of my sons used to come with me. He used to carry a few coppers. For a paper, perhaps, to see how the M.C.C. was getting on overseas. Otherwise my name was good. Besides, I was a very busy man.

MCCANN. I didn't know you had any sons.

GOLDBERG. But of course. I've been a family man.

MCCANN. How many did you have?
GOLDBERG. I lost my last two—in an accident. But the first, the first grew up to be a fine boy.
MCCANN. What's he doing now?
GOLDBERG. I often wonder that myself. Yes. Emanuel. A quiet fellow. He never said much. Timmy I used to call him.
MCCANN. Emanuel?
GOLDBERG. That's right. Manny.
MCCANN. Manny?
GOLDBERG. Sure. It's short for Emanuel.
MCCANN. I thought you called him Timmy.
GOLDBERG. I did.
MCCANN. What about this, Nat? Isn't it about time someone came in?
GOLDBERG. McCann, what are you so nervous about? Pull yourself together. Everywhere you go these days it's like a funeral.
MCCANN. That's true.
GOLDBERG. True? Of course it's true. It's more than true. It's a fact.
MCCANN. You may be right.
GOLDBERG. What is it, McCann? You don't trust me like you did in the old days?
MCCANN. Sure I trust you, Nat.
GOLDBERG. I'm glad. But why is it that before you do a job you're all over the place, and when you're doing the job you're as cool as a whistle?
MCCANN. I don't know, Nat. I'm just all right once I know what I'm doing. When I know what I'm doing, I'm all right.
GOLDBERG. Well, you do it very well.
MCCANN. Thank you, Nat.
GOLDBERG. As a matter of fact I was talking about you only the other day. I gave you a very good name.
MCCANN. That was kind of you, Nat.
GOLDBERG. And then this job came up out of the blue. Natu-

rally they approached me to take care of it. And you know who I asked for?

MCCANN. Who?

GOLDBERG. You.

MCCANN. That was very good of you, Nat.

GOLDBERG. No, it was nothing. You're a capable man, McCann.

MCCANN. That's a great compliment, Nat, coming from a man in your position.

GOLDBERG. Well, I've got a position, I won't deny it.

MCCANN. You certainly have.

GOLDBERG. I would never deny that I had a position.

MCCANN. And what a position!

GOLDBERG. It's not a thing I would deny.

MCCANN. Yes, it's true, you've done a lot for me. I appreciate it.

GOLDBERG. Say no more.

MCCANN. You've always been a true Christian.

GOLDBERG. In a way.

MCCANN. No, I just thought I'd tell you that I appreciate it.

GOLDBERG. It's unnecessary to recapitulate.

MCCANN. You're right there.

GOLDBERG. Quite unnecessary.

Pause. MCCANN *leans forward.*

MCCANN. Hey Nat, just one thing. . . .

GOLDBERG. What now?

MCCANN. This job—no, listen—this job, is it going to be like anything we've ever done before?

GOLDBERG. Tch, tch, tch.

MCCANN. No, just tell me that. Just that, and I won't ask any more.

GOLDBERG *sighs, stands, goes behind the table, ponders, looks at* MCCANN, *and then speaks in a quiet, fluent, official tone.*

GOLDBERG. The main issue is a singular issue and quite distinct from your previous work. Certain elements, however, might well approximate in points of procedure to some of your other activities. All is dependent on the attitude of our subject. At all events, McCann, I can assure you that the assignment will be carried out and the mission accomplished with no excessive aggravation to you or myself. Satisfied?

MCCANN. Sure. Thank you, Nat.

MEG *enters, left.*

GOLDBERG. Ah, Mrs. Boles?

MEG. Yes?

GOLDBERG. We spoke to your husband last night. Perhaps he mentioned us? We heard that you kindly let rooms for gentlemen. So I brought my friend along with me. We were after a nice place, you understand. So we came to you. I'm Mr. Goldberg and this is Mr. McCann.

MEG. Very pleased to meet you.

They shake hands.

GOLDBERG. We're pleased to meet you, too.

MEG. That's very nice.

GOLDBERG. You're right. How often do you meet someone it's a pleasure to meet?

MCCANN. Never.

GOLDBERG. But today it's different. How are you keeping, Mrs. Boles?

MEG. Oh, very well, thank you.

GOLDBERG. Yes? Really?

MEG. Oh yes, really.

GOLDBERG. I'm glad. What do you say, McCann? Oh, Mrs. Boles, would you mind if my friend went into your kitchen and had a little gargle?

MEG (*to* MCCANN). Why, have you got a sore throat?

MCCANN. Er—yes.

MEG. Do you want some salt?

MCCANN. Salt?

MEG. Salt's good.
GOLDBERG. Good? It's wonderful. Go on, off you go, McCann.
MC CANN. Where is the kitchen?
MEG. Over there. (MC CANN *goes to the kitchen*.) There's some salt on the shelf.

MC CANN *exits*. GOLDBERG *sits at the table, right.*

GOLDBERG. So you can manage to put us up, eh, Mrs. Boles?
MEG. Well, it would have been easier last week.
GOLDBERG. Last week.
MEG. Or next week.
GOLDBERG. Next week.
MEG. Yes.
GOLDBERG. How many have you got here at the moment?
MEG. Just one at the moment.
GOLDBERG. Just one?
MEG. Yes. Just one. Until you came.
GOLDBERG. And your husband, of course?
MEG. Yes, but he sleeps with me.
GOLDBERG. What does he do, your husband?
MEG. He's a deck-chair attendant.
GOLDBERG. Oh, very nice.
MEG. Yes, he's out in all weathers.

She begins to take her purchases from her bag.

GOLDBERG. Of course. And your guest? Is he a man?
MEG. A man?
GOLDBERG. Or a woman?
MEG. No. A man.
GOLDBERG. Been here long?
MEG. He's been here about a year now.
GOLDBERG. Oh yes. A resident. What's his name?
MEG. Stanley Webber.
GOLDBERG. Oh yes? Does he work here?
MEG. He used to work. He used to be a pianist. In a concert party on the pier.

GOLDBERG. Oh yes? On the pier, eh? Does he play a nice piano?

MEG. Oh, lovely. (*She sits at the table.*) He once gave a concert.

GOLDBERG. Oh? Where?

MEG (*falteringly*). In . . . a big hall. His father gave him champagne. But then they locked the place up and he couldn't get out. The caretaker had gone home. So he had to wait until the morning before he could get out. (*With confidence.*) They were very grateful. (*Pause.*) And then they all wanted to give him a tip. And so he took the tip. And then he got a fast train and he came down here.

GOLDBERG. Really?

MEG. Oh yes. Straight down.

Pause.

MEG. I wish he could have played tonight.

GOLDBERG. Why tonight?

MEG. It's his birthday today.

GOLDBERG. His birthday?

MEG. Yes. Today. But I'm not going to tell him until tonight.

GOLDBERG. Doesn't he know it's his birthday?

MEG. He hasn't mentioned it.

GOLDBERG (*thoughtfully*). Well, well, well. Tell me. Are you going to have a party?

MEG. A party?

GOLDBERG. Weren't you going to have one?

MEG (*her eyes wide*). No.

GOLDBERG. Well, of course, you must have one. (*He stands.*) We'll have a party, eh? What do you say?

MEG. Oh yes!

GOLDBERG. Sure. We'll give him a party. Leave it to me.

MEG. Oh, that's wonderful, Mr. Gold—

GOLDBERG. Berg.

MEG. Berg.

GOLDBERG. You like the idea?
MEG. Oh, I'm so glad you came today.
GOLDBERG. If we hadn't come today we'd have come tomorrow. Still, I'm glad we came today. Just in time for his birthday.
MEG. I wanted to have a party. But you must have people for a party.
GOLDBERG. And now you've got McCann and me. McCann's the life and soul of any party.

    MCCANN *enters from the kitchen.*

MEG. I'll invite Lulu this afternoon. (*To* MCCANN.) We're going to have a party tonight.
MCCANN. What?
GOLDBERG. There's a gentleman living here, McCann, who's got a birthday today, and he's forgotten all about it. So we're going to remind him. We're going to give him a party.
MCCANN. Oh, is that a fact?
MEG. Tonight.
GOLDBERG. Tonight. Did you have a good gargle?
MCCANN. Yes, thanks.
MEG. I'll put on my party dress.
GOLDBERG. And I'll get some bottles.
MEG. Oh, this is going to cheer Stanley up. It will. He's been down in the dumps lately.
GOLDBERG. We'll bring him out of himself.
MEG. I hope I look nice in my dress.
GOLDBERG. Madam, you'll look like a tulip.
MEG. What colour?
GOLDBERG. Er—well, I'll have to see the dress first.
MCCANN. Could I go up to my room?
MEG. Oh, I've put you both together. Do you mind being both together?
GOLDBERG. I don't mind. Do you mind, McCann?
MCCANN. No.
MEG. What time shall we have the party?

GOLDBERG. Nine o'clock.
MCCANN (*at the door*). Is this the way?
MEG (*rising*). I'll show you. If you don't mind coming upstairs.
GOLDBERG. With a tulip? It's a pleasure.

> MEG *and* GOLDBERG *exit laughing, followed by* MC-CANN. STANLEY *appears at the window. He enters by the back door. He goes to the door on the left, opens it and listens. Silence. He walks to the table. He stands. He sits, as* MEG *enters. She crosses and hangs her shopping bag on a hook. He lights a match and watches it burn.*

STANLEY. Who is it?
MEG. The two gentlemen.
STANLEY. What two gentlemen?
MEG. The ones that were coming. I just took them to their room. They were thrilled with their room.
STANLEY. They've come?
MEG. They're very nice, Stan.
STANLEY. Why didn't they come last night?
MEG. They said the beds were wonderful.
STANLEY. Who are they?
MEG (*sitting*). They're very nice, Stanley.
STANLEY. I said, who are they?
MEG. I've told you, the two gentlemen.
STANLEY. I didn't think they'd come.

> *He rises and walks to the window.*

MEG. They have. They were here when I came in.
STANLEY. What do they want here?
MEG. They want to stay.
STANLEY. How long for?
MEG. They didn't say.
STANLEY (*turning*). But why here? Why not somewhere else?
MEG. This house is on the list.

STANLEY (*coming down*). What are they called? What are their names?

MEG. Oh, Stanley, I can't remember.

STANLEY. They told you, didn't they? Or didn't they tell you?

MEG. Yes, they. . . .

STANLEY. Then what are they? Come on. Try to remember.

MEG. Why, Stan? Do you know them?

STANLEY. How do I know if I know them until I know their names?

MEG. Well . . . he told me, I remember.

STANLEY. Well?

She thinks.

MEG. Gold—something.

STANLEY. Goldsomething?

MEG. Yes. Gold. . . .

STANLEY. Yes?

MEG. Goldberg.

STANLEY. Goldberg?

MEG. That's right. That was one of them.

STANLEY *slowly sits at the table, left.*

Do you know them?

STANLEY *does not answer.*

Stan, they won't wake you up, I promise. I'll tell them they must be quiet.

STANLEY *sits still.*

They won't be here long, Stan. I'll still bring you up your early morning tea.

STANLEY *sits still.*

You mustn't be sad today. It's your birthday.

A pause.

STANLEY (*dumbly*). Uh?
MEG. It's your birthday, Stan. I was going to keep it a secret until tonight.
STANLEY. No.
MEG. It is. I've brought you a present. (*She goes to the sideboard, picks up the parcel, and places it on the table in front of him.*) Here. Go on. Open it.
STANLEY. What's this?
MEG. It's your present.
STANLEY. This isn't my birthday, Meg.
MEG. Of course it is. Open your present.

He stares at the parcel, slowly stands, and opens it. He takes out a boy's drum.

STANLEY (*flatly*). It's a drum. A boy's drum.
MEG (*tenderly*). It's because you haven't got a piano. (*He stares at her, then turns and walks towards the door, left.*) Aren't you going to give me a kiss? (*He turns sharply, and stops. He walks back towards her slowly. He stops at her chair, looking down upon her. Pause. His shoulders sag, he bends and kisses her on the cheek.*) There are some sticks in there. (STANLEY *looks into the parcel. He takes out two drumsticks. He taps them together. He looks at her.*)
STANLEY. Shall I put it round my neck?

She watches him, uncertainly. He hangs the drum around his neck, taps it gently with the sticks, then marches round the table, beating it regularly. MEG, *pleased, watches him. Still beating it regularly, he begins to go round the table a second time. Halfway round the beat becomes erratic, uncontrolled.* MEG *expresses dismay. He arrives at her chair, banging the drum, his face and the drumbeat now savage and possessed.*

Curtain

Act Two

MCCANN *is sitting at the table tearing a sheet of newspaper into five equal strips. It is evening. After a few moments* STANLEY *enters from the left. He stops upon seeing* MC-CANN, *and watches him. He then walks towards the kitchen, stops, and speaks.*

STANLEY. Evening.
MCCANN. Evening.

> *Chuckles are heard from outside the back door, which is open.*

STANLEY. Very warm tonight. (*He turns towards the back door, and back.*) Someone out there?

> MCCANN *tears another length of paper.* STANLEY *goes into the kitchen and pours a glass of water. He drinks it looking through the hatch. He puts the glass down, comes out of the kitchen and walks quickly towards the door, left.* MCCANN *rises and intercepts him.*

MCCANN. I don't think we've met.
STANLEY. No, we haven't.
MCCANN. My name's McCann.
STANLEY. Staying here long?
MCCANN. Not long. What's your name?
STANLEY. Webber.
MCCANN. I'm glad to meet you, sir. (*He offers his hand.* STANLEY *takes it, and* MCCANN *holds the grip.*) Many happy returns of the day. (STANLEY *withdraws his hand. They face each other.*) Were you going out?
STANLEY. Yes.
MCCANN. On your birthday?

STANLEY. Yes. Why not?
MC CANN. But they're holding a party here for you tonight.
STANLEY. Oh really? That's unfortunate.
MC CANN. Ah no. It's very nice.

Voices from outside the back door.

STANLEY. I'm sorry. I'm not in the mood for a party tonight.
MC CANN. Oh, is that so? I'm sorry.
STANLEY. Yes, I'm going out to celebrate quietly, on my own.
MC CANN. That's a shame.

They stand.

STANLEY. Well, if you'd move out of my way—
MC CANN. But everything's laid on. The guests are expected.
STANLEY. Guests? What guests?
MC CANN. Myself for one. I had the honour of an invitation.

MC CANN *begins to whistle "The Mountains of Morne".*

STANLEY (*moving away*). I wouldn't call it an honour, would you? It'll just be another booze-up.

STANLEY *joins* MC CANN *in whistling "The Mountains of Morne". During the next five lines the whistling is continuous, one whistling while the other speaks, and both whistling together.*

MC CANN. But it is an honour.
STANLEY. I'd say you were exaggerating.
MC CANN. Oh no. I'd say it was an honour.
STANLEY. I'd say that was plain stupid.
MC CANN. Oh no.

They stare at each other.

STANLEY. Who are the other guests?
MC CANN. A young lady.

STANLEY. Oh yes? And. . . . ?
MCCANN. My friend.
STANLEY. Your friend?
MCCANN. That's right. It's all laid on.

    STANLEY *walks round the table towards the door.* MC-CANN *meets him.*

STANLEY. Excuse me.
MCCANN. Where are you going?
STANLEY. I want to go out.
MCCANN. Why don't you stay here?

    STANLEY *moves away, to the right of the table.*

STANLEY. So you're down here on holiday?
MCCANN. A short one. (STANLEY *picks up a strip of paper.* MCCANN *moves in.*) Mind that.
STANLEY. What is it?
MCCANN. Mind it. Leave it.
STANLEY. I've got a feeling we've met before.
MCCANN. No we haven't.
STANLEY. Ever been anywhere near Maidenhead?
MCCANN. No.
STANLEY. There's a Fuller's teashop. I used to have my tea there.
MCCANN. I don't know it.
STANLEY. And a Boots Library. I seem to connect you with the High Street.
MCCANN. Yes?
STANLEY. A charming town, don't you think?
MCCANN. I don't know it.
STANLEY. Oh no. A quiet, thriving community. I was born and brought up there. I lived well away from the main road.
MCCANN. Yes?

    Pause.

STANLEY. You're here on a short stay?
MCCANN. That's right.
STANLEY. You'll find it very bracing.
MCCANN. Do you find it bracing?
STANLEY. Me? No. But you will. (*He sits at the table.*) I like it here, but I'll be moving soon. Back home. I'll stay there too, this time. No place like home. (*He laughs.*) I wouldn't have left, but business calls. Business called, and I had to leave for a bit. You know how it is.
MCCANN (*sitting at the table, left*). You in business?
STANLEY. No. I think I'll give it up. I've got a small private income, you see. I think I'll give it up. Don't like being away from home. I used to live very quietly—played records, that's about all. Everything delivered to the door. Then I started a little private business, in a small way, and it compelled me to come down here—kept me longer than I expected. You never get used to living in someone else's house. Don't you agree? I lived so quietly. You can only appreciate what you've had when things change. That's what they say, isn't it? Cigarette?
MCCANN. I don't smoke.

STANLEY *lights a cigarette. Voices from the back.*

STANLEY. Who's out there?
MCCANN. My friend and the man of the house.
STANLEY. You know what? To look at me, I bet you wouldn't think I'd led such a quiet life. The lines on my face, eh? It's the drink. Been drinking a bit down here. But what I mean is . . . you know how it is . . . away from your own . . . all wrong, of course . . . I'll be all right when I get back . . . but what I mean is, the way some people look at me you'd think I was a different person. I suppose I have changed, but I'm still the same man that I always was. I mean, you wouldn't think, to look at me, really . . . I mean, not really, that I was the sort of bloke to—to cause any trouble, would you?

(MC CANN *looks at him.*) Do you know what I mean?
MC CANN. No. (*As* STANLEY *picks up a strip of paper.*) Mind that.
STANLEY (*quickly*). Why are you down here?
MC CANN. A short holiday.
STANLEY. This is a ridiculous house to pick on. (*He rises.*)
MC CANN. Why?
STANLEY. Because it's not a boarding house. It never was.
MC CANN. Sure it is.
STANLEY. Why did you choose this house?
MC CANN. You know, sir, you're a bit depressed for a man on his birthday.
STANLEY (*sharply*). Why do you call me sir?
MC CANN. You don't like it?
STANLEY (*to the table*). Listen. Don't call me sir.
MC CANN. I won't, if you don't like it.
STANLEY (*moving away*). No. Anyway, this isn't my birthday.
MC CANN. No?
STANLEY. No. It's not till next month.
MC CANN. Not according to the lady.
STANLEY. Her? She's crazy. Round the bend.
MC CANN. That's a terrible thing to say.
STANLEY (*to the table*). Haven't you found that out yet? There's a lot you don't know. I think someone's leading you up the garden path.
MC CANN. Who would do that?
STANLEY (*leaning across the table*). That woman is mad!
MC CANN. That's slander.
STANLEY. And you don't know what you're doing.
MC CANN. Your cigarette is near that paper.

Voices from the back.

STANLEY. Where the hell are they? (*Stubbing his cigarette.*) Why don't they come in? What are they doing out there?

MCCANN. You want to steady yourself.

STANLEY *crosses to him and grips his arm.*

STANLEY (*urgently*). Look—
MCCANN. Don't touch me.
STANLEY. Look. Listen a minute.
MCCANN. Let go my arm.
STANLEY. Look. Sit down a minute.
MCCANN (*savagely, hitting his arm*). Don't do that!

STANLEY *backs across the stage, holding his arm.*

STANLEY. Listen. You knew what I was talking about before, didn't you?
MCCANN. I don't know what you're at at all.
STANLEY. It's a mistake! Do you understand?
MCCANN. You're in a bad state, man.
STANLEY (*whispering, advancing*). Has he told you anything? Do you know what you're here for? Tell me. You needn't be frightened of me. Or hasn't he told you?
MCCANN. Told me what?
STANLEY (*hissing*). I've explained to you, damn you, that all those years I lived in Basingstoke I never stepped outside the door.
MCCANN. You know, I'm flabbergasted with you.
STANLEY (*reasonably*). Look. You look an honest man. You're being made a fool of, that's all. You understand? Where do you come from?
MCCANN. Where do you think?
STANLEY. I know Ireland very well. I've many friends there. I love that country and I admire and trust its people. I trust them. They respect the truth and they have a sense of humour. I think their policemen are wonderful. I've been there. I've never seen such sunsets. What about coming out to have a drink with me? There's a pub down the road serves draught Guinness. Very difficult to get in these parts— (*He breaks off. The voices draw nearer.* GOLDBERG *and* PETEY *enter from the back door.*)

GOLDBERG (*as he enters*). A mother in a million. (*He sees* STANLEY.) Ah.
PETEY. Oh hullo, Stan. You haven't met Stanley, have you, Mr. Goldberg?
GOLDBERG. I haven't had the pleasure.
PETEY. Oh well, this is Mr. Goldberg, this is Mr. Webber.
GOLDBERG. Pleased to meet you.
PETEY. We were just getting a bit of air in the garden.
GOLDBERG. I was telling Mr. Boles about my old mum. What days. (*He sits at the table, right.*) Yes. When I was a youngster, of a Friday, I used to go for a walk down the canal with a girl who lived down my road. A beautiful girl. What a voice that bird had! A nightingale, my word of honour. Good? Pure? She wasn't a Sunday school teacher for nothing. Anyway, I'd leave her with a little kiss on the cheek—I never took liberties—we weren't like the young men these days in those days. We knew the meaning of respect. So I'd give her a peck and I'd bowl back home. Humming away I'd be, past the children's playground. I'd tip my hat to the toddlers, I'd give a helping hand to a couple of stray dogs, everything came natural. I can see it like yesterday. The sun falling behind the dog stadium. Ah! (*He leans back contentedly.*)
MC CANN. Like behind the town hall.
GOLDBERG. What town hall?
MC CANN. In Carrikmacross.
GOLDBERG. There's no comparison. Up the street, into my gate, inside the door, home. "Simey!" my old mum used to shout, "quick before it gets cold." And there on the table what would I see? The nicest piece of gefilte fish you could wish to find on a plate.
MC CANN. I thought your name was Nat.
GOLDBERG. She called me Simey.
PETEY. Yes, we all remember our childhood.
GOLDBERG. Too true. Eh, Mr. Webber, what do you say? Childhood. Hot water bottles. Hot milk. Pancakes. Soap suds. What a life.

Pause.

PETEY (*rising from the table*). Well, I'll have to be off.
GOLDBERG. Off?
PETEY. It's my chess night.
GOLDBERG. You're not staying for the party?
PETEY. No, I'm sorry, Stan. I didn't know about it till just now. And we've got a game on. I'll try and get back early.
GOLDBERG. We'll save some drink for you, all right? Oh, that reminds me. You'd better go and collect the bottles.
MCCANN. Now?
GOLDBERG. Of course, now. Time's getting on. Round the corner, remember? Mention my name.
PETEY. I'm coming your way.
GOLDBERG. Beat him quick and come back, Mr. Boles.
PETEY. Do my best. See you later, Stan.

PETEY *and* MCCANN *go out, left.* STANLEY *moves to the centre.*

GOLDBERG. A warm night.
STANLEY (*turning*). Don't mess me about!
GOLDBERG. I beg your pardon?
STANLEY (*moving downstage*). I'm afraid there's been a mistake. We're booked out. Your room is taken. Mrs. Boles forgot to tell you. You'll have to find somewhere else.
GOLDBERG. Are you the manager here?
STANLEY. That's right.
GOLDBERG. Is it a good game?
STANLEY. I run the house. I'm afraid you and your friend will have to find other accommodation.
GOLDBERG (*rising*). Oh, I forgot, I must congratulate you on your birthday. (*Offering his hand.*) Congratulations.
STANLEY (*ignoring hand*). Perhaps you're deaf.
GOLDBERG. No, what makes you think that? As a matter of fact, every single one of my senses is at its peak. Not bad

going, eh? For a man past fifty. But a birthday, I always feel, is a great occasion, taken too much for granted these days. What a thing to celebrate—birth! Like getting up in the morning. Marvellous! Some people don't like the idea of getting up in the morning. I've heard them. Getting up in the morning, they say, what is it? Your skin's crabby, you need a shave, your eyes are full of muck, your mouth is like a boghouse, the palms of your hands are full of sweat, your nose is clogged up, your feet stink, what are you but a corpse waiting to be washed? Whenever I hear that point of view I feel cheerful. Because I know what it is to wake up with the sun shining, to the sound of the lawnmower, all the little birds, the smell of the grass, church bells, tomato juice—

STANLEY. Get out.

Enter MCCANN, *with bottles.*

Get that drink out. These are unlicensed premises.

GOLDBERG. You're in a terrible humour today, Mr. Webber. And on your birthday too, with the good lady getting her strength up to give you a party.

MCCANN *puts the bottles on the sideboard.*

STANLEY. I told you to get those bottles out.

GOLDBERG. Mr. Webber, sit down a minute.

STANLEY. Let me—just make this clear. You don't bother me. To me, you're nothing but a dirty joke. But I have a responsibility towards the people in this house. They've been down here too long. They've lost their sense of smell. I haven't. And nobody's going to take advantage of them while I'm here. (*A little less forceful.*) Anyway, this house isn't your cup of tea. There's nothing here for you, from any angle. So why don't you just go, without any more fuss?

GOLDBERG. Mr. Webber, sit down.

STANLEY. It's no good starting any kind of trouble.

GOLDBERG. Sit down.

STANLEY. Why should I?
GOLDBERG. If you want to know the truth, Webber, you're beginning to get on my breasts.
STANLEY. Really? Well, that's—
GOLDBERG. Sit down.
STANLEY. No.

GOLDBERG *sighs, and sits at the table right.*

GOLDBERG. McCann.
MCCANN. Nat?
GOLDBERG. Ask him to sit down.
MCCANN. Yes, Nat. (MCCANN *moves to* STANLEY.) Do you mind sitting down?
STANLEY. Yes, I do mind.
MCCANN. Yes now, but—it'd be better if you did.
STANLEY. Why don't you sit down?
MCCANN. No, not me—you.
STANLEY. No thanks.

Pause.

MCCANN. Nat.
GOLDBERG. What?
MCCANN. He won't sit down.
GOLDBERG. Well, ask him.
MCCANN. I've asked him.
GOLDBERG. Ask him again.
MCCANN (*to* STANLEY). Sit down.
STANLEY. Why?
MCCANN. You'd be more comfortable.
STANLEY. So would you.

Pause.

MCCANN. All right. If you will I will.
STANLEY. You first.

MCCANN *slowly sits at the table, left.*

MCCANN. Well?

STANLEY. Right. Now you've both had a rest you can get out!
MCCANN (*rising*). That's a dirty trick! I'll kick the shite out of him!
GOLDBERG (*rising*). No! I have stood up.
MCCANN. Sit down again!
GOLDBERG. Once I'm up I'm up.
STANLEY. Same here.
MCCANN (*moving to* STANLEY). You've made Mr. Goldberg stand up.
STANLEY (*his voice rising*). It'll do him good!
MCCANN. Get in that seat.
GOLDBERG. McCann.
MCCANN. Get down in that seat!
GOLDBERG (*crossing to him*). Webber. (*Quietly.*) SIT DOWN. (*Silence.* STANLEY *begins to whistle "The Mountains of Morne". He strolls casually to the chair at the table. They watch him. He stops whistling. Silence. He sits.*)
STANLEY. You'd better be careful.
GOLDBERG. Webber, what were you doing yesterday?
STANLEY. Yesterday?
GOLDBERG. And the day before. What did you do the day before that?
STANLEY. What do you mean?
GOLDBERG. Why are you wasting everybody's time, Webber? Why are you getting in everybody's way?
STANLEY. Me? What are you—
GOLDBERG. I'm telling you, Webber. You're a washout. Why are you getting on everybody's wick? Why are you driving that old lady off her conk?
MCCANN. He likes to do it!
GOLDBERG. Why do you behave so badly, Webber? Why do you force that old man out to play chess?
STANLEY. Me?
GOLDBERG. Why do you treat that young lady like a leper? She's not the leper, Webber!

STANLEY. What the—
GOLDBERG. What did you wear last week, Webber? Where do you keep your suits?
MCCANN. Why did you leave the organization?
GOLDBERG. What would your old mum say, Webber?
MCCANN. Why did you betray us?
GOLDBERG. You hurt me, Webber. You're playing a dirty game.
MCCANN. That's a Black and Tan fact.
GOLDBERG. Who does he think he is?
MCCANN. Who do you think you are?
STANLEY. You're on the wrong horse.
GOLDBERG. When did you come to this place?
STANLEY. Last year.
GOLDBERG. Where did you come from?
STANLEY. Somewhere else.
GOLDBERG. Why did you come here?
STANLEY. My feet hurt!
GOLDBERG. Why did you stay?
STANLEY. I had a headache!
GOLDBERG. Did you take anything for it?
STANLEY. Yes.
GOLDBERG. What?
STANLEY. Fruit salts!
GOLDBERG. Enos or Andrews?
STANLEY. En— An—
GOLDBERG. Did you stir properly? Did they fizz?
STANLEY. Now, now, wait, you—
GOLDBERG. Did they fizz? Did they fizz or didn't they fizz?
MCCANN. He doesn't know!
GOLDBERG. You don't know. What's happened to your memory, Webber? When did you last have a bath?
STANLEY. I have one every—
GOLDBERG. Don't lie.
MCCANN. You betrayed the organization. I know him!
STANLEY. You don't!
GOLDBERG. What can you see without your glasses?

STANLEY. Anything.
GOLDBERG. Take off his glasses.

> MCCANN *snatches his glasses and as* STANLEY *rises, reaching for them, takes his chair downstage centre, below the table,* STANLEY *stumbling as he follows.* STANLEY *clutches the chair and stays bent over it.*

Webber, you're a fake. (*They stand on each side of the chair.*) When did you last wash up a cup?
STANLEY. The Christmas before last.
GOLDBERG. Where?
STANLEY. Lyons Corner House.
GOLDBERG. Which one?
STANLEY. Marble Arch.
GOLDBERG. Where was your wife?
STANLEY. In—
GOLDBERG. Answer.
STANLEY (*turning, crouched*). What wife?
GOLDBERG. What have you done with your wife?
MCCANN. He's killed his wife!
GOLDBERG. Why did you kill your wife?
STANLEY (*sitting, his back to the audience*). What wife?
MCCANN. How did he kill her?
GOLDBERG. How did you kill her?
MCCANN. You throttled her.
GOLDBERG. With arsenic.
MCCANN. There's your man!
GOLDBERG. Where's your old mum?
STANLEY. In the sanatorium.
MCCANN. Yes!
GOLDBERG. Why did you never get married?
MCCANN. She was waiting at the porch.
GOLDBERG. You skedaddled from the wedding.
MCCANN. He left her in the lurch.
GOLDBERG. You left her in the pudding club.
MCCANN. She was waiting at the church.
GOLDBERG. Webber! Why did you change your name?

STANLEY. I forgot the other one.
GOLDBERG. What's your name now?
STANLEY. Joe Soap.
GOLDBERG. You stink of sin.
MC CANN. I can smell it.
GOLDBERG. Do you recognise an external force?
STANLEY. What?
GOLDBERG. Do you recognise an external force?
MC CANN. That's the question!
GOLDBERG. Do you recognise an external force, responsible for you, suffering for you?
STANLEY. It's late.
GOLDBERG. Late! Late enough! When did you last pray?
MC CANN. He's sweating!
GOLDBERG. When did you last pray?
MC CANN. He's sweating!
GOLDBERG. Is the number 846 possible or necessary?
STANLEY. Neither.
GOLDBERG. Wrong! Is the number 846 possible or necessary?
STANLEY. Both.
GOLDBERG. Wrong! It's necessary but not possible.
STANLEY. Both.
GOLDBERG. Wrong! Why do you think the number 846 is necessarily possible?
STANLEY. Must be.
GOLDBERG. Wrong! It's only necessarily necessary! We admit possibility only after we grant necessity. It is possible because necessary but by no means necessary through possibility. The possibility can only be assumed after the proof of necessity.
MC CANN. Right!
GOLDBERG. Right? Of course right! We're right and you're wrong, Webber, all along the line.
MC CANN. All along the line!
GOLDBERG. Where is your lechery leading you?
MC CANN. You'll pay for this.

GOLDBERG. You stuff yourself with dry toast.
MCCANN. You contaminate womankind.
GOLDBERG. Why don't you pay the rent?
MCCANN. Mother defiler!
GOLDBERG. Why do you pick your nose?
MCCANN. I demand justice!
GOLDBERG. What's your trade?
MCCANN. What about Ireland?
GOLDBERG. What's your trade?
STANLEY. I play the piano.
GOLDBERG. How many fingers do you use?
STANLEY. No hands!
GOLDBERG. No society would touch you. Not even a building society.
MCCANN. You're a traitor to the cloth.
GOLDBERG. What do you use for pyjamas?
STANLEY. Nothing.
GOLDBERG. You verminate the sheet of your birth.
MCCANN. What about the Albigensenist heresy?
GOLDBERG. Who watered the wicket in Melbourne?
MCCANN. What about the blessed Oliver Plunkett?
GOLDBERG. Speak up Webber. Why did the chicken cross the road?
STANLEY. He wanted to—he wanted to—he wanted to. . . .
MCCANN. He doesn't know!
GOLDBERG. Why did the chicken cross the road?
STANLEY. He wanted to—he wanted to. . . .
GOLDBERG. Why did the chicken cross the road?
STANLEY. He wanted. . . .
MCCANN. He doesn't know. He doesn't know which came first!
GOLDBERG. Which came first?
MCCANN. Chicken? Egg? Which came first?
GOLDBERG and MCCANN. Which came first? Which came first? Which came first?

  STANLEY *screams.*

GOLDBERG. He doesn't know. Do you know your own face?
MCCANN. Wake him up. Stick a needle in his eye.
GOLDBERG. You're a plague, Webber. You're an overthrow.
MCCANN. You're what's left!
GOLDBERG. But we've got the answer to you. We can sterilise you.
MCCANN. What about Drogheda?
GOLDBERG. Your bite is dead. Only your pong is left.
MCCANN. You betrayed our land.
GOLDBERG. You betray our breed.
MCCANN. Who are you, Webber?
GOLDBERG. What makes you think you exist?
MCCANN. You're dead.
GOLDBERG. You're dead. You can't live, you can't think, you can't love. You're dead. You're a plague gone bad. There's no juice in you. You're nothing but an odour!

Silence. They stand over him. He is crouched in the chair. He looks up slowly and kicks GOLDBERG *in the stomach.* GOLDBERG *falls.* STANLEY *stands.* MCCANN *seizes a chair and lifts it above his head.* STANLEY *seizes a chair and covers his head with it.* MCCANN *and* STANLEY *circle.*

GOLDBERG. Steady, McCann.
STANLEY (*circling*). Uuuuuhhhhh!
MCCANN. Right, Judas.
GOLDBERG (*rising*). Steady, McCann.
MCCANN. Come on!
STANLEY. Uuuuuuuhhhhh!
MCCANN. He's sweating.
GOLDBERG. Easy, McCann.
MCCANN. The bastard sweatpig is sweating.

A loud drumbeat off left, descending the stairs. GOLDBERG *takes the chair from* STANLEY. *They put the chairs down. They stop still. Enter* MEG, *in evening dress, holding sticks and drum.*

MEG. I brought the drum down. I'm dressed for the party.
GOLDBERG. Wonderful.
MEG. You like my dress?
GOLDBERG. Wonderful. Out of this world.
MEG. I know. My father gave it to me. (*Placing drum on table.*) Doesn't it make a beautiful noise?
GOLDBERG. It's a fine piece of work. Maybe Stan'll play us a little tune afterwards.
MEG. Oh yes. Will you, Stan?
STANLEY. Could I have my glasses?
GOLDBERG. Ah yes. (*He holds his hand out to* MCCANN. MCCANN *passes him his glasses.*) Here they are. (*He holds them out for* STANLEY, *who reaches for them.*) Here they are. (STANLEY *takes them.*) Now. What have we got here? Enough to scuttle a liner. We've got four bottles of Scotch and one bottle of Irish.
MEG. Oh, Mr. Goldberg, what should I drink?
GOLDBERG. Glasses, glasses first. Open the Scotch, McCann.
MEG (*at the sideboard*). Here's my very best glasses in here.
MCCANN. I don't drink Scotch.
GOLDBERG. You drink that one.
MEG (*bringing the glasses*). Here they are.
GOLDBERG. Good. Mrs. Boles, I think Stanley should pour the toast, don't you?
MEG. Oh yes. Come on, Stanley. (STANLEY *walks slowly to the table.*) Do you like my dress, Mr. Goldberg?
GOLDBERG. It's out on its own. Turn yourself round a minute. I used to be in the business. Go on, walk up there.
MEG. Oh no.
GOLDBERG. Don't be shy. (*He slaps her bottom.*)
MEG. Oooh!
GOLDBERG. Walk up the boulevard. Let's have a look at you. What a carriage. What's your opinion, McCann? Like a Countess, nothing less. Madam, now turn about and promenade to the kitchen. What a deportment!
MCCANN (*to* STANLEY). You can pour my Irish too.
GOLDBERG. You look like a gladiola.

MEG. Stan, what about my dress?

GOLDBERG. One for the lady, one for the lady. Now madam —your glass.

MEG. Thank you.

GOLDBERG. Lift your glasses, ladies and gentlemen. We'll drink a toast.

MEG. Lulu isn't here.

GOLDBERG. It's past the hour. Now—who's going to propose the toast? Mrs. Boles, it can only be you.

MEG. Me?

GOLDBERG. Who else?

MEG. But what do I say?

GOLDBERG. Say what you feel. What you honestly feel. (MEG *looks uncertain.*) It's Stanley's birthday. Your Stanley. Look at him. Look at him and it'll come. Wait a minute, the light's too strong. Let's have proper lighting. McCann, have you got your torch?

MCCANN (*bringing a small torch from his pocket*). Here.

GOLDBERG. Switch out the light and put on your torch. (MCCANN *goes to the door, switches off the light, comes back, shines the torch on* MEG. *Outside the window there is still a faint light.*) Not on the lady, on the gentleman! You must shine it on the birthday boy. (MCCANN *shines the torch in* STANLEY'S *face.*) Now, Mrs. Boles, it's all yours.

Pause.

MEG. I don't know what to say.

GOLDBERG. Look at him. Just look at him.

MEG. Isn't the light in his eyes?

GOLDBERG. No, no. Go on.

MEG. Well—it's very, very nice to be here tonight, in my house, and I want to propose a toast to Stanley, because it's his birthday, and he's lived here for a long while now, and he's my Stanley now. And I think he's a good boy, although sometimes he's bad. (*An appreciative laugh from* GOLDBERG.) And he's the only Stanley I know, and

I know him better than all the world, although he doesn't think so. (*"Hear—hear" from* GOLDBERG.) Well, I could cry because I'm so happy, having him here and not gone away, on his birthday, and there isn't anything I wouldn't do for him, and all you good people here tonight. . . . (*She sobs.*)

GOLDBERG. Beautiful! A beautiful speech. Put the light on, McCann. (MC CANN *goes to the door.* STANLEY *remains still.*) That was a lovely toast. (*The light goes on.* LULU *enters from the door, left.* GOLDBERG *comforts* MEG.) Buck up now. Come on, smile at the birdy. That's better. We've got to drink yet. Ah, look who's here.

MEG. Lulu.

GOLDBERG. How do you do, Lulu? I'm Nat Goldberg. Stanley, a drink for your guest. You just missed the toast, my dear, and what a toast.

LULU. Did I?

GOLDBERG. Stanley, a drink for your guest. Stanley. (STANLEY *hands a glass to* LULU.) Right. Now raise your glasses. Everyone standing up? No, not you, Stanley. You must sit down.

MC CANN. Yes, that's right. He must sit down.

GOLDBERG. You don't mind sitting down a minute? We're going to drink to you.

MEG. Come on!

STANLEY *sits in a chair at the table.*

GOLDBERG. Right. Now Stanley's sat down. (*Taking the stage.*) Well, I want to say first that I've never been so touched to the heart as by the toast we've just heard. How often, in this day and age, do you come across real, true warmth? Once in a lifetime. Until a few minutes ago, ladies and gentlemen, I, like all of you, was asking the same question. What's happened to the love, the bonhomie, the unashamed expression of affection of the day before yesterday, that our mums taught us in the nursery?

MC CANN. Gone with the wind.

GOLDBERG. That's what I thought, until today. I believe in a good laugh, a day's fishing, a bit of gardening. I was very proud of my old greenhouse, made out of my own spit and faith. That's the sort of man I am. Not size but quality. A little Austin, tea in Fullers, a library book from Boots, and I'm satisfied. But just now, I say just now, the lady of the house said her piece and I for one am knocked over by the sentiments she expressed. Lucky is the man who's at the receiving end, that's what I say. (*Pause.*) How can I put it to you? We all wander on our tod through this world. It's a lonely pillow to kip on. Right!
LULU (*admiringly*). Right!
GOLDBERG. Agreed. But tonight, Lulu, McCann, we've known a great fortune. We've heard a lady extend the sum total of her devotion, in all its pride, plume and peacock, to a member of her own living race. Stanley, my heartfelt congratulations. I wish you, on behalf of us all, a happy birthday. I'm sure you've never been a prouder man than you are today. Mazoltov! And may we only meet at Simchahs! (LULU *and* MEG *applaud.*) Turn out the light, McCann, while we drink the toast.
LULU. That was a wonderful speech.

> MC CANN *switches out the light, comes back, and shines the torch in* STANLEY'S *face. The light outside the window is fainter.*

GOLDBERG. Lift your glasses. Stanley—happy birthday.
MC CANN. Happy birthday.
LULU. Happy birthday.
MEG. Many happy returns of the day, Stan.
GOLDBERG. And well over the fast.

> *They all drink.*

MEG (*kissing him*). Oh, Stanny. . . .
GOLDBERG. Lights!
MC CANN. Right! (*He switches on the lights.*)
MEG. Clink my glass, Stan.

LULU. Mr. Goldberg—
GOLDBERG. Call me Nat.
MEG (*to* MC CANN). You clink my glass.
LULU (*to* GOLDBERG). You're empty. Let me fill you up.
GOLDBERG. It's a pleasure.
LULU. You're a marvellous speaker, Nat, you know that? Where did you learn to speak like that?
GOLDBERG. You liked it, eh?
LULU. Oh yes!
GOLDBERG. Well, my first chance to stand up and give a lecture was at the Ethical Hall, Bayswater. A wonderful opportunity. I'll never forget it. They were all there that night. Charlotte Street was empty. Of course, that's a good while ago.
LULU. What did you speak about?
GOLDBERG. The Necessary and the Possible. It went like a bomb. Since then I always speak at weddings.

> STANLEY *is still.* GOLDBERG *sits left of the table.* MEG *joins* MC CANN *downstage, right,* LULU *is downstage, left.* MC CANN *pours more Irish from the bottle, which he carries, into his glass.*

MEG. Let's have some of yours.
MC CANN. In that?
MEG. Yes.
MC CANN. Are you used to mixing them?
MEG. No.
MC CANN. Sit down. Give me your glass.

> MEG *sits on a shoe-box, downstage, right.* LULU, *at the table, pours more drink for* GOLDBERG *and herself, and gives* GOLDBERG *his glass.*

GOLDBERG. Thank you.
MEG (*to* MC CANN). Do you think I should?
GOLDBERG. Lulu, you're a big bouncy girl. Come and sit on my lap.
MC CANN. Why not?

LULU. Do you think I should?
GOLDBERG. Try it.
MEG (*sipping*). Very nice.
LULU. I'll bounce up to the ceiling.
MCCANN. I don't know how you can mix that stuff.
GOLDBERG. Take a chance.
MEG (*to* MCCANN). Sit down on this stool.

    LULU *sits on* GOLDBERG'S *lap*.

MCCANN. This?
GOLDBERG. Comfortable?
LULU. Yes, thanks.
MCCANN (*sitting*). It's comfortable.
GOLDBERG. You know, there's a lot in your eyes.
LULU. And in yours, too.
GOLDBERG. Do you think so?
LULU (*giggling*). Go on!
MCCANN (*to* MEG). Where'd you get it?
MEG. My father gave it to me.
LULU. I didn't know I was going to meet you here tonight.
MCCANN (*to* MEG). Ever been to Carrikmacross?
MEG (*drinking*). I've been to King's Cross.
LULU. You came right out of the blue, you know that?
GOLDBERG (*as she moves*). Mind how you go. You're cracking a rib.
MEG (*standing*). I want to dance! (LULU *and* GOLDBERG *look into each other's eyes*. MCCANN *drinks*. MEG *crosses to* STANLEY). Stanley. Dance. (STANLEY *sits still*. MEG *dances round the room alone, then comes back to* MCCANN, *who fills her glass. She sits.*)
LULU (*to* GOLDBERG). Shall I tell you something?
GOLDBERG. What?
LULU. I trust you.
GOLDBERG (*lifting his glass*). Gesundheit.
LULU. Have you got a wife?
GOLDBERG. I had a wife. What a wife. Listen to this. Friday, of an afternoon, I'd take myself for a little constitutional,

down over the park. Eh, do me a favour, just sit on the table a minute, will you? (LULU *sits on the table. He stretches and continues.*) A little constitutional. I'd say hullo to the little boys, the little girls—I never made distinctions—and then back I'd go, back to my bungalow with the flat roof. "Simey," my wife used to shout, "quick, before it gets cold!" And there on the table what would I see? The nicest piece of rollmop and pickled cucumber you could wish to find on a plate.

LULU. I thought your name was Nat.

GOLDBERG. She called me Simey.

LULU. I bet you were a good husband.

GOLDBERG. You should have seen her funeral.

LULU. Why?

GOLDBERG (*draws in his breath and wags head*). What a funeral.

MEG (*to* MCCANN). My father was going to take me to Ireland once. But then he went away by himself.

LULU (*to* GOLDBERG). Do you think you knew me when I was a little girl?

GOLDBERG. Were you a nice little girl?

LULU. I was.

MEG. I don't know if he went to Ireland.

GOLDBERG. Maybe I played piggy-back with you.

LULU. Maybe you did.

MEG. He didn't take me.

GOLDBERG. Or pop goes the weasel.

LULU. Is that a game?

GOLDBERG. Sure it's a game!

MCCANN. Why didn't he take you to Ireland?

LULU. You're tickling me!

GOLDBERG. You should worry.

LULU. I've always liked older men. They can soothe you.

They embrace.

MCCANN. I know a place. Roscrea. Mother Nolan's.

MEG. There was a night-light in my room, when I was a little girl.

MCCANN. One time I stayed there all night with the boys. Singing and drinking all night.

MEG. And my Nanny used to sit up with me, and sing songs to me.

MCCANN. And a plate of fry in the morning. Now where am I?

MEG. My little room was pink. I had a pink carpet and pink curtains, and I had musical boxes all over the room. And they played me to sleep. And my father was a very big doctor. That's why I never had any complaints. I was cared for, and I had little sisters and brothers in other rooms, all different colours.

MCCANN. Tullamore, where are you?

MEG (*to* MCCANN). Give us a drop more.

MCCANN (*filling her glass and singing*). Glorio, Glorio, to the bold Fenian men!

MEG. Oh, what a lovely voice.

GOLDBERG. Give us a song, McCann.

LULU. A love song!

MCCANN (*reciting*). The night that poor Paddy was stretched, the boys they all paid him a visit.

GOLDBERG. A love song!

MCCANN (*in a full voice, sings*)

   Oh, the Garden of Eden has vanished, they say,
   But I know the lie of it still.
   Just turn to the left at the foot of Ben Clay
   And stop when halfway to Coote Hill.
   It's there you will find it, I know sure enough,
   And it's whispering over to me:
   Come back, Paddy Reilly, to Bally-James-Duff,
   Come home, Paddy Reilly, to me!

LULU (*to* GOLDBERG). You're the dead image of the first man I ever loved.

GOLDBERG. It goes without saying.

ACT II] THE BIRTHDAY PARTY 63

MEG (*rising*). I want to play a game!
GOLDBERG. A game?
LULU. What game?
MEG. Any game.
LULU (*jumping up*). Yes, let's play a game.
GOLDBERG. What game?
MC CANN. Hide and seek.
LULU. Blind man's buff.
MEG. Yes!
GOLDBERG. You want to play blind man's buff?
LULU and MEG. Yes!
GOLDBERG. All right. Blind man's buff. Come on! Everyone up! (*Rising.*) McCann. Stanley—Stanley!
MEG. Stanley. Up.
GOLDBERG. What's the matter with him?
MEG (*bending over him*). Stanley, we're going to play a game. Oh, come on, don't be sulky, Stan.

STANLEY *rises*. MC CANN *rises*.

GOLDBERG. Right! Now—who's going to be blind first?
LULU. Mrs. Boles.
MEG. Not me.
GOLDBERG. Of course you.
MEG. Who, me?
LULU (*taking her scarf from her neck*). Here you are.
MC CANN. How do you play this game?
LULU (*tying her scarf round* MEG's *eyes*). Haven't you ever played blind man's buff? Keep still, Mrs. Boles. You mustn't be touched. But you can't move after she's blind. You must stay where you are after she's blind. And if she touches you then you become blind. Turn round. How many fingers am I holding up?
MEG. I can't see.
LULU. Right.
GOLDBERG. Right! Everyone move about. McCann. Stanley. Now stop. Now still. Off you go!

STANLEY *is downstage, right,* MEG *moves about the room.* GOLDBERG *fondles* LULU *at arm's length.* MEG *touches* MCCANN.

MEG. Caught you!
LULU. Take off your scarf.
MEG. What lovely hair!
LULU (*untying the scarf*). There.
MEG. It's you!
GOLDBERG. Put it on, McCann.
LULU (*tying it on* MCCANN). There. Turn round. How many fingers am I holding up?
MCCANN. I don't know.
GOLDBERG. Right! Everyone move about. Right. Stop! Still!

MCCANN *begins to move.*

MEG. Oh, this is lovely!
GOLDBERG. Quiet! Tch, tch, tch. Now—all move again. Stop! Still!

MCCANN *moves about.* GOLDBERG *fondles* LULU *at arm's length.* MCCANN *draws near* STANLEY. *He stretches his arm and touches* STANLEY'S *glasses.*

MEG. It's Stanley!
GOLDBERG (*to* LULU). Enjoying the game?
MEG. It's your turn, Stan.

MCCANN *takes off the scarf.*

MCCANN (*to* STANLEY). I'll take your glasses.

MCCANN *takes* STANLEY'S *glasses.*

MEG. Give me the scarf.
GOLDBERG (*holding* LULU). Tie his scarf, Mrs. Boles.
MEG. That's what I'm doing.
LULU (*to* GOLDBERG). Kiss me. (*They kiss.*)
MEG (*to* STANLEY). Can you see my nose?
GOLDBERG. He can't. Ready? Right! Everyone move. Stop! And still!

ACT II] THE BIRTHDAY PARTY 65

STANLEY *stands blindfold.* MCCANN *backs slowly across the stage to the left. He breaks* STANLEY'S *glasses, snapping the frames.* MEG *is downstage, left,* LULU *and* GOLDBERG *upstage centre, close together.* STANLEY *begins to move, very slowly, across the stage to the left.* MCCANN *picks up the drum and places it sideways in* STANLEY'S *path.* STANLEY *walks into the drum and falls over with his foot caught in it.*

MEG. Ooh!
GOLDBERG. Sssh!

STANLEY *rises. He begins to move towards* MEG, *dragging the drum on his foot. He reaches her and stops. His hands move towards her and they reach her throat. He begins to strangle her.* MCCANN *and* GOLDBERG *rush forward and throw him off.*

Blackout

There is now no light at all through the window. The stage is in darkness.

LULU. The lights!
GOLDBERG. What's happened?
LULU. The lights!
MCCANN. Wait a minute.
GOLDBERG. Where is he?
MCCANN. Let go of me!
LULU. Someone's touching me!
GOLDBERG. Who's this?
MEG. It's me!
MCCANN. Where is he?
MEG. Why has the light gone out?
GOLDBERG. Where's your torch? (MCCANN *shines the torch in* GOLDBERG'S *face.*) Not on me! (MCCANN *shifts the torch. It is knocked from his hand and falls. It goes out.*)
MCCANN. My torch!
LULU. Oh God!

GOLDBERG. Where's your torch? Pick up your torch!
MCCANN. I can't find it.
LULU. Hold me. Hold me.
GOLDBERG. Get down on your knees. Help him find the torch.
LULU. I can't.
MCCANN. It's gone.
MEG. Why has the light gone out?
GOLDBERG. Everyone quiet! Help him find the torch.

> *Silence. Grunts from* MCCANN *and* GOLDBERG *on their knees. Suddenly there is a sharp, sustained rat-a-tat with a stick on the side of the drum from the back of the room. Silence. Whimpers from* LULU.

GOLDBERG. Over here. McCann!
MCCANN. Here.
GOLDBERG. Come to me, come to me. Easy. Over there.

> GOLDBERG *and* MCCANN *move up left of the table.* STANLEY *moves down right of the table.* LULU *suddenly perceives him moving towards her, screams and faints.* GOLDBERG *and* MCCANN *turn and stumble against each other.*

GOLDBERG. What is it?
MCCANN. Who's that?
GOLDBERG. What is it?

> *In the darkness* STANLEY *picks up* LULU *and places her on the table.*

MEG. It's Lulu!

> GOLDBERG *and* MCCANN *move downstage, right.*

GOLDBERG. Where is she?
MCCANN. She fell.
GOLDBERG. Where?
MCCANN. About here.
GOLDBERG. Help me pick her up.

ACT II] THE BIRTHDAY PARTY 67

MCCANN (*moving downstage, left*). I can't find her.
GOLDBERG. She must be somewhere.
MCCANN. She's not here.
GOLDBERG (*moving downstage, left*). She must be.
MCCANN. She's gone.

> MCCANN *finds the torch on the floor, shines it on the table and* STANLEY. LULU *is lying spread-eagled on the table,* STANLEY *bent over her.* STANLEY, *as soon as the torchlight hits him, begins to giggle.* GOLDBERG *and* MCCANN *move towards him. He backs, giggling, the torch on his face. They follow him upstage, left. He backs against the hatch, giggling. The torch draws closer. His giggle rises and grows as he flattens himself against the wall. Their figures converge upon him.*

Curtain

Act Three

The next morning. PETEY *enters, left, with a newspaper and sits at the table. He begins to read.* MEG'S *voice comes through the kitchen hatch.*

MEG. Is that you, Stan? (*Pause.*) Stanny?
PETEY. Yes?
MEG. Is that you?
PETEY. It's me.
MEG (*appearing at the hatch*). Oh, it's you. I've run out of cornflakes.
PETEY. Well, what else have you got?
MEG. Nothing.
PETEY. Nothing?
MEG. Just a minute. (*She leaves the hatch and enters by the kitchen door.*) You got your paper?
PETEY. Yes.
MEG. Is it good?
PETEY. Not bad.
MEG. The two gentlemen had the last of the fry this morning.
PETEY. Oh, did they?
MEG. There's some tea in the pot though. (*She pours tea for him.*) I'm going out shopping in a minute. Get you something nice.
PETEY. Good.
MEG. Oh, I must sit down a minute. (*Sits at the table, right.*)
PETEY. How are you then, this morning?
MEG. I've got a splitting headache.
PETEY (*reading*). You slept like a log last night.
MEG. Did I?
PETEY. Why don't you have a walk down to the shops? It's fresh out. It'll clear your head.
MEG. Will it?

ACT III] THE BIRTHDAY PARTY 69

PETEY. Bound to.
MEG. I will then. Did I sleep like a log?
PETEY. Dead out.
MEG. I must have been tired. (*She looks about the room and sees the broken drum in the fireplace.*) Oh, look. (*She rises and picks it up.*) The drum's broken. (PETEY *looks up.*) Why is it broken?
PETEY. I don't know.

She hits it with her hand.

MEG. It still makes a noise.
PETEY. You can always get another one.
MEG (*sadly*). It was probably broken in the party. I don't remember it being broken though, in the party. (*She puts it down.*) What a shame.
PETEY. You can always get another one, Meg.
MEG. Well, at least he did have it on his birthday, didn't he? Like I wanted him to.
PETEY (*reading*). Yes.
MEG. Have you seen him down yet? (PETEY *does not answer.*) Petey.
PETEY. What?
MEG. Have you seen him down?
PETEY. Who?
MEG. Stanley.
PETEY. No.
MEG. Nor have I. That boy should be up. He's late for his breakfast.
PETEY. There isn't any breakfast.
MEG. Yes, but he doesn't know that. I'm going to call him.
PETEY (*quickly*). No, don't do that, Meg. Let him sleep.
MEG. But you say he stays in bed too much.
PETEY. Let him sleep . . . this morning. Leave him.
MEG. I've been up once, with his cup of tea. But Mr. McCann opened the door. He said they were talking. He said he'd made him one. He must have been up early. I don't know what they were talking about. I was surprised.

Because Stanley's usually fast asleep when I wake him. But he wasn't this morning. I heard him talking. (*Pause.*) Do you think they know each other? I think they're old friends. Stanley had a lot of friends. I know he did. (*Pause.*) I didn't give him his tea. He'd already had one. I came down again and went on with my work. Then, after a bit, they came down to breakfast. Stanley must have gone to sleep again.

Pause.

PETEY. When are you going to do your shopping, Meg?
MEG. Yes, I must. (*Collecting the bag.*) I've got a rotten headache. (*She goes to the back door, stops suddenly and turns.*) Did you see what's outside this morning?
PETEY. What?
MEG. That big car.
PETEY. Yes.
MEG. It wasn't there yesterday. Did you . . . did you have a look inside it?
PETEY. I had a peep.
MEG (*coming down tensely, and whispering*). Is there anything in it?
PETEY. In it?
MEG. Yes.
PETEY. What do you mean, in it?
MEG. Inside it.
PETEY. What sort of thing?
MEG. Well . . . I mean . . . is there . . . is there a wheelbarrow in it?
PETEY. A wheelbarrow?
MEG. Yes.
PETEY. I didn't see one.
MEG. You didn't? Are you sure?
PETEY. What would Mr. Goldberg want with a wheelbarrow?
MEG. Mr. Goldberg?
PETEY. It's his car.
MEG (*relieved*). His car? Oh, I didn't know it was his car.

PETEY. Of course it's his car.
MEG. Oh, I feel better.
PETEY. What are you on about?
MEG. Oh, I do feel better.
PETEY. You go and get a bit of air.
MEG. Yes, I will. I will. I'll go and get the shopping. (*She goes towards the back door. A door slams upstairs. She turns.*) It's Stanley! He's coming down—what am I going to do about his breakfast? (*She rushes into the kitchen.*) Petey, what shall I give him? (*She looks through the hatch.*) There's no cornflakes. (*They both gaze at the door. Enter* GOLDBERG. *He halts at the door, as he meets their gaze, then smiles.*)
GOLDBERG. A reception committee!
MEG. Oh, I thought it was Stanley.
GOLDBERG. You find a resemblance?
MEG. Oh no. You look quite different.
GOLDBERG (*coming into the room*). Different build, of course.
MEG (*entering from the kitchen*). I thought he was coming down for his breakfast. He hasn't had his breakfast yet.
GOLDBERG. Your wife makes a very nice cup of tea, Mr. Boles, you know that?
PETEY. Yes, she does sometimes. Sometimes she forgets.
MEG. Is he coming down?
GOLDBERG. Down? Of course he's coming down. On a lovely sunny day like this he shouldn't come down? He'll be up and about in next to no time. (*He sits at the table.*) And what a breakfast he's going to get.
MEG. Mr. Goldberg.
GOLDBERG. Yes?
MEG. I didn't know that was your car outside.
GOLDBERG. You like it?
MEG. Are you going to go for a ride?
GOLDBERG (*to* PETEY). A smart car, eh?
PETEY. Nice shine on it all right.
GOLDBERG. What is old is good, take my tip. There's room

there. Room in the front, and room in the back. (*He strokes the teapot.*) The pot's hot. More tea, Mr. Boles?
PETEY. No thanks.
GOLDBERG (*pouring tea*). That car? That car's never let me down.
MEG. Are you going to go for a ride?
GOLDBERG (*ruminatively*). And the boot. A beautiful boot. There's just room . . . for the right amount.
MEG. Well, I'd better be off now. (*She moves to the back door, and turns.*) Petey, when Stanley comes down. . . .
PETEY. Yes?
MEG. Tell him I won't be long.
PETEY. I'll tell him.
MEG (*vaguely*). I won't be long. (*She exits.*)
GOLDBERG (*sipping his tea*). A good woman. A charming woman. My mother was the same. My wife was identical.
PETEY. How is he this morning?
GOLDBERG. Who?
PETEY. Stanley. Is he any better?
GOLDBERG (*a little uncertainly*). Oh . . . a little better, I think, a little better. Of course, I'm not really qualified to say, Mr. Boles. I mean, I haven't got the . . . the qualifications. The best thing would be if someone with the proper . . . mnn . . . qualifications . . . was to have a look at him. Someone with a few letters after his name. It makes all the difference.
PETEY. Yes.
GOLDBERG. Anyway, Dermot's with him at the moment. He's . . . keeping him company.
PETEY. Dermot?
GOLDBERG. Yes.
PETEY. It's a terrible thing.
GOLDBERG (*sighs*). Yes. The birthday celebration was too much for him.
PETEY. What came over him?
GOLDBERG (*sharply*). What came over him? Breakdown, Mr. Boles. Pure and simple. Nervous breakdown.

PETEY. But what brought it on so suddenly?

GOLDBERG (*rising, and moving upstage*). Well, Mr. Boles, it can happen in all sorts of ways. A friend of mine was telling me about it only the other day. We'd both been concerned with another case—not entirely similar, of course, but . . . quite alike, quite alike. (*He pauses.*) Anyway, he was telling me, you see, this friend of mine, that sometimes it happens gradual—day by day it grows and grows and grows . . . day by day. And then other times it happens all at once. Poof! Like that! The nerves break. There's no guarantee how it's going to happen, but with certain people . . . it's a foregone conclusion.

PETEY. Really?

GOLDBERG. Yes. This friend of mine—he was telling me about it—only the other day. (*He stands uneasily for a moment, then brings out a cigarette case and takes a cigarette.*) Have an Abdullah.

PETEY. No, no, I don't take them.

GOLDBERG. Once in a while I treat myself to a cigarette. An Abdullah, perhaps, or a . . . (*He snaps his fingers.*)

PETEY. What a night. (GOLDBERG *lights his cigarette with a lighter.*) Came in the front door and all the lights were out. Put a shilling in the slot, came in here and the party was over.

GOLDBERG (*coming downstage*). You put a shilling in the slot?

PETEY. Yes.

GOLDBERG. And the lights came on.

PETEY. Yes, then I came in here.

GOLDBERG (*with a short laugh*). I could have sworn it was a fuse.

PETEY (*continuing*). There was dead silence. Couldn't hear a thing. So I went upstairs and your friend—Dermot—met me on the landing. And he told me.

GOLDBERG (*sharply*). Who?

PETEY. Your friend—Dermot.

GOLDBERG (*heavily*). Dermot. Yes. (*He sits.*)

PETEY. They get over it sometimes though, don't they? I mean, they can recover from it, can't they?

GOLDBERG. Recover? Yes, sometimes they recover, in one way or another.

PETEY. I mean, he might have recovered by now, mightn't he?

GOLDBERG. It's conceivable. Conceivable.

  PETEY *rises and picks up the teapot and cup.*

PETEY. Well, if he's no better by lunchtime I'll go and get hold of a doctor.

GOLDBERG (*briskly*). It's all taken care of, Mr. Boles. Don't worry yourself.

PETEY (*dubiously*). What do you mean? (*A door slams upstairs. They look towards the door. Enter* MCCANN *with two suitcases.*) Oh, it's you. All packed up?

  PETEY *takes the teapot and cups into the kitchen.* MCCANN *crosses left and puts down the suitcases. He goes up to the window and looks out.*

GOLDBERG. Well? (MCCANN *does not answer.*) McCann. I asked you well.

MCCANN (*without turning*). Well what?

GOLDBERG. What's what? (MCCANN *does not answer.*) What is what?

MCCANN (*turning to look at* GOLDBERG, *grimly*). I'm not going up there again.

GOLDBERG. Why not?

MCCANN. I'm not going up there again.

GOLDBERG. What's going on now?

MCCANN (*moving down*). He's quiet now. He stopped all that . . . talking a while ago.

  PETEY *appears at the kitchen hatch, unnoticed.*

GOLDBERG. When will he be ready?

MCCANN (*sullenly*). You can go up yourself next time.

GOLDBERG. What's the matter with you?

MCCANN (*quietly*). I gave him. . . .

GOLDBERG. What?
MCCANN. I gave him his glasses.
GOLDBERG. Wasn't he glad to get them back?
MCCANN. The frames are bust.
GOLDBERG. How did that happen?
MCCANN. He tried to fit the eyeholes into his eyes. I left him doing it.
PETEY (*at the kitchen door*). There's some Sellotape somewhere. We can stick them together.

GOLDBERG *and* MCCANN *turn to see him. Pause.*

GOLDBERG. Sellotape? No, no, that's all right, Mr. Boles. It'll keep him quiet for the time being, keep his mind off other things.
PETEY (*moving downstage*). What about a doctor?
GOLDBERG. It's all taken care of.

MCCANN *moves over right to the shoe-box, and takes out a brush and brushes his shoes.*

PETEY (*moves to the table*). I think he needs one.
GOLDBERG. I agree with you. It's all taken care of. We'll give him a bit of time to settle down, and then I'll take him to Monty.
PETEY. You're going to take him to a doctor?
GOLDBERG (*staring at him*). Sure. Monty.

Pause. MCCANN *brushes his shoes.* PETEY *sits, left, at the table.*

So Mrs. Boles has gone out to get us something nice for lunch?
PETEY. That's right.
GOLDBERG. Unfortunately we may be gone by then.
PETEY. Will you?
GOLDBERG. By then we may be gone.
MCCANN (*breaking in*). You know that girl?
GOLDBERG. What girl?
MCCANN. That girl had nightmares in the night.
GOLDBERG. Those weren't nightmares.

MCCANN. No?
GOLDBERG (*irritably*). I said no.
MCCANN. How do you know?
GOLDBERG. I got up. I went to see what was the matter.
MCCANN. I didn't know that.
GOLDBERG (*sharply*). It may be that you didn't know that. Nevertheless, that's what happened.
MCCANN. Well, what was the matter?
GOLDBERG. Nothing. Nothing at all. She was just having a bit of a sing-song.
MCCANN. A sing-song?
GOLDBERG (*to* PETEY). Sure. You know how young girls sing. She was singing.
MCCANN. So what happened then?
GOLDBERG. I joined in. We had a few songs. Yes. We sang a few of the old ballads and then she went to bye-byes.

PETEY *rises.*

PETEY. Well, I think I'll see how my peas are getting on, in the meantime.
GOLDBERG. The meantime?
PETEY. While we're waiting.
GOLDBERG. Waiting for what? (PETEY *walks towards the back door.*) Aren't you going back to the beach?
PETEY. No, not yet. Give me a call when he comes down, will you, Mr. Goldberg?
GOLDBERG (*earnestly*). You'll have a crowded beach today . . . on a day like this. They'll be lying on their backs, swimming out to sea. My life. What about the deck-chairs? Are the deck-chairs ready?
PETEY. I put them all out this morning.
GOLDBERG. But what about the tickets? Who's going to take the tickets?
PETEY. That's all right. That'll be all right, Mr. Goldberg. Don't you worry about that. I'll be back.

He exits. GOLDBERG *rises, goes to the window and looks*

after him. MC CANN *crosses to the table, left, sits, picks up the paper and begins to tear it into strips.*

GOLDBERG. Is everything ready?
MC CANN. Sure.

GOLDBERG *walks heavily, brooding, to the table. He sits right of it noticing what* MC CANN *is doing.*

GOLDBERG. Stop doing that!
MC CANN. What?
GOLDBERG. Why do you do that all the time? It's childish, it's pointless. It's without a solitary point.
MC CANN. What's the matter with you today?
GOLDBERG. Questions, questions. Stop asking me so many questions. What do you think I am?

MC CANN *studies him. He then folds the paper, leaving the strips inside.*

MC CANN. Well?

Pause. GOLDBERG *leans back in the chair, his eyes closed.*

MC CANN. Well?
GOLDBERG (*with fatigue*). Well what?
MC CANN. What's what?
GOLDBERG. Yes, what is what. . . .
MC CANN. Do we wait or do we go and get him?
GOLDBERG (*slowly*). You want to go and get him?
MC CANN. I want to get it over.
GOLDBERG. That's understandable.
MC CANN. So do we wait or do we—?
GOLDBERG (*interrupting*). I don't know why, but I feel knocked out. I feel a bit . . . It's uncommon for me.
MC CANN. Is that so?
GOLDBERG. It's unusual.
MC CANN (*rising swiftly and going behind* GOLDBERG'S *chair. Hissing*). Let's finish and go. Let's get it over and go.

Get the thing done. Let's finish the bloody thing. Let's get the thing done and go!

Pause.

Will I go up?

Pause.

Nat!

GOLDBERG *sits humped.* MCCANN *slips to his side.*

Simey!

GOLDBERG (*opening his eyes, regarding* MCCANN). What —did—you—call—me?
MCCANN. Who?
GOLDBERG (*murderously*). Don't call me that! (*He seizes* MCCANN *by the throat.*) NEVER CALL ME THAT!
MCCANN (*writhing*). Nat, Nat, Nat, NAT! I called you Nat. I was asking you, Nat. Honest to God. Just a question, that's all, just a question, do you see, do you follow me?
GOLDBERG (*jerking him away*). What question?
MCCANN. Will I go up?
GOLDBERG (*violently*). Up? I thought you weren't going to go up there again?
MCCANN. What do you mean? Why not?
GOLDBERG. You said so!
MCCANN. I never said that!
GOLDBERG. No?
MCCANN (*from the floor, to the room at large*). Who said that? I never said that! I'll go up now!

He jumps up and rushes to the door, left.

GOLDBERG. Wait!

He stretches his arms to the arms of the chair.

Come here.

MCCANN *approaches him very slowly.*

I want your opinion. Have a look in my mouth.

He opens his mouth wide.

Take a good look.

MC CANN *looks.*

You know what I mean?

MC CANN *peers.*

You know what? I've never lost a tooth. Not since the day I was born. Nothing's changed. (*He gets up.*) That's why I've reached my position, McCann. Because I've always been as fit as a fiddle. All my life I've said the same. Play up, play up, and play the game. Honour thy father and thy mother. All along the line. Follow the line, the line, McCann, and you can't go wrong. What do you think, I'm a self-made man? No! I sat where I was told to sit. I kept my eye on the ball. School? Don't talk to me about school. Top in all subjects. And for why? Because I'm telling you, I'm telling you, follow my line? Follow my mental? Learn by heart. Never write down a thing. No. And don't go too near the water. And you'll find—that what I say is true.
Because I believe that the world . . . (*Vacant.*). . . .
Because I believe that the world . . . (*Desperate.*). . . .
BECAUSE I BELIEVE THAT THE WORLD . . . (*Lost.*). . . .

He sits in chair.

Sit down, McCann, sit here where I can look at you.

MC CANN *kneels in front of the table.*

(*Intensely, with growing certainty.*) My father said to me, Benny, Benny, he said, come here. He was dying. I knelt down. By him day and night. Who else was there? Forgive, Benny, he said, and let live. Yes, Dad. Go home to your wife. I will, Dad. Keep an eye open for low-lives, for schnorrers and for layabouts. He didn't mention names. I lost my life in the service of others, he said, I'm not ashamed. Do your duty and keep your observations. Always bid good morning to the neighbours. Never, never forget your family, for they are the rock, the constitution and the core! If you're ever in any difficulties Uncle Barney will see you in the clear. I knelt down. (*He kneels, facing* MC CANN.) I swore on the good book. And I knew the word I had to remember—Respect! Because McCann—(*Gently.*) Seamus—who came before your father? His father. And who came before him? Before him? . . . (*Vacant—triumphant.*) Who came before your father's father but your father's father's mother! Your great-grangranny.

Silence. He slowly rises.

And that's why I've reached my position, McCann. Because I've always been as fit as a fiddle. My motto. Work hard and play hard. Not a day's illness. (*He emits a high-pitched wheeze-whine. He looks round.*) What was that?
MC CANN. What?
GOLDBERG. I heard something.
MC CANN. What was it?
GOLDBERG. A noise. A funny noise.
MC CANN. That was you.
GOLDBERG. Me?
MC CANN. Sure.
GOLDBERG (*interested*). What, you heard it too?
MC CANN. I did.
GOLDBERG. It was me, eh? (*A slight chuckle.*) Huh. What did I do?
MC CANN. You gave . . . you let out a class of a wheeze, like.
GOLDBERG. Go on! (*He laughs. They both laugh. Then suddenly, quickly, anxiously.*) Where's your spoon? You got your spoon?
MC CANN (*producing it*). Here.
GOLDBERG. Test me. (*He opens his mouth and sticks out his*

tongue.) Here. (MC CANN *places the spoon on* GOLD-BERG'S *tongue.*) Aaaahhh! Aaaaahhhh!

MC CANN. Perfect condition.

GOLDBERG. You really mean that?

MC CANN. My word of honour.

GOLDBERG. So now you can understand why I occupy such a position, eh?

MC CANN. I can, of course.

  GOLDBERG *laughs. They both laugh.*

GOLDBERG (*stopping*). All the same, give me a blow. (*Pause.*) Blow in my mouth.

  MC CANN *stands, puts his hands on his knees, bends, and blows in* GOLDBERG'S *mouth.*

One for the road.

  MC CANN *blows again in his mouth.* GOLDBERG *breathes deeply, shakes his head, and bounds from the chair.*

Right. We're here. Wait a minute, just a minute. You got everything packed?

MC CANN. I have.

GOLDBERG. The expander?

MC CANN. Yes.

GOLDBERG. Fetch it to me.

MC CANN. Now?

GOLDBERG. At once.

  MC CANN *goes to the suitcase and takes out a chest expander. He gives it to* GOLDBERG, *who pulls it playfully, masterfully, bearing down on* MC CANN. *They both chuckle.* GOLDBERG *pulls it to full stretch. It breaks. He smiles.*

What did I tell you?

  He throws it at MC CANN. *Enter* LULU, *left.*

Well, look who's here.

MCCANN *looks at them, and goes to the door.*

MCCANN (*at the door*). I'll give you five minutes. (*He exits with the expander.*)
GOLDBERG. Come over here.
LULU. What's going to happen?
GOLDBERG. Come over here.
LULU. No, thank you.
GOLDBERG. What's the matter? You got the needle to Uncle Natey?
LULU. I'm going.
GOLDBERG. Have a game of pontoon first, for old time's sake.
LULU. I've had enough games.
GOLDBERG. A girl like you, at your age, at your time of health, and you don't take to games?
LULU. You're very smart.
GOLDBERG. Anyway, who says you don't take to them?
LULU. Do you think I'm like all the other girls?
GOLDBERG. Are all the other girls like that, too?
LULU. I don't know about any other girls.
GOLDBERG. Nor me. I've never touched another woman.
LULU (*distressed*). What would my father say, if he knew? And what would Eddie say?
GOLDBERG. Eddie?
LULU. He was my first love, Eddie was. And whatever happened, it was pure. With him! He didn't come into my room at night with a briefcase!
GOLDBERG. Who opened the briefcase, me or you?
LULU. You got round me. It was only because I was so upset by last night.
GOLDBERG. Lulu, schmulu, let bygones be bygones, do me a turn. Kiss and make up.
LULU. I wouldn't touch you.
GOLDBERG. And today I'm leaving.
LULU. You're leaving?
GOLDBERG. Today.

LULU (*with growing anger*). You used me for a night. A passing fancy.
GOLDBERG. Who used who?
LULU. You made use of me by cunning when my defences were down.
GOLDBERG. Who took them down?
LULU. That's what you did. You quenched your ugly thirst. You took advantage of me when I was overwrought. I wouldn't do those things again, not even for a Sultan!
GOLDBERG. One night doesn't make a harem.
LULU. You taught me things a girl shouldn't know before she's been married at least three times!
GOLDBERG. Now you're a jump ahead! What are you complaining about?

Enter MCCANN *quickly.*

LULU. You didn't appreciate me for myself. You took all those liberties only to satisfy your appetite.
GOLDBERG. Now you're giving me indigestion.
LULU. And after all that had happened. An old woman nearly killed and a man gone mad—How can I go back behind that counter now? Oh Nat, why did you do it?
GOLDBERG. You wanted me to do it, Lulula, so I did it.
MCCANN. That's fair enough.
LULU (*turning*). Oh!
MCCANN (*advancing*). You had a long sleep, Miss.
LULU (*backing upstage left*). Me?
MCCANN. Your sort, you spend too much time in bed.
LULU. What do you mean?
MCCANN. Have you got anything to confess?
LULU. What?
MCCANN (*savagely*). Confess!
LULU. Confess what?
MCCANN. Down on your knees and confess!
LULU. What does he mean?
GOLDBERG. Confess. What can you lose?
LULU. What, to him?

GOLDBERG. He's only been unfrocked six months.
MCCANN. Kneel down, woman, and tell me the latest!
LULU (*retreating to the back door*). I've seen everything that's happened. I know what's going on. I've got a pretty shrewd idea.
MCCANN (*advancing*). I've seen you hanging about the Rock of Cashel, profaning the soil with your goings-on. Out of my sight!
LULU. I'm going.

> *She exits.* MCCANN *goes to the door, left, and goes out. He ushers in* STANLEY, *who is dressed in striped trousers, black jacket, and white collar. He carries a bowler hat in one hand and his broken glasses in the other. He is clean-shaven.* MCCANN *follows and closes the door.* GOLDBERG *meets* STANLEY, *seats him in a chair, right, and puts his hat on the table.*

GOLDBERG. How are you, Stan?

Pause.

Are you feeling any better?

Pause.

What's the matter with your glasses?

> GOLDBERG *bends to look.*

They're broken. A pity.

> STANLEY *stares blankly at the floor.*

MCCANN (*at the table*). He looks better, doesn't he?
GOLDBERG. Much better.
MCCANN. A new man.
GOLDBERG. You know what we'll do?
MCCANN. What?
GOLDBERG. We'll buy him another pair.

> *They begin to woo him, gently and with relish. During*

ACT III] THE BIRTHDAY PARTY 85

the following sequence STANLEY *shows no reaction. He remains, with no movement, where he sits.*

MCCANN. Out of our own pockets.
GOLDBERG. It goes without saying. Between you and me, Stan, it's about time you had a new pair of glasses.
MCCANN. You can't see straight.
GOLDBERG. It's true. You've been cockeyed for years.
MCCANN. Now you're even more cockeyed.
GOLDBERG. He's right. You've gone from bad to worse.
MCCANN. Worse than worse.
GOLDBERG. You need a long convalescence.
MCCANN. A change of air.
GOLDBERG. Somewhere over the rainbow.
MCCANN. Where angels fear to tread.
GOLDBERG. Exactly.
MCCANN. You're in a rut.
GOLDBERG. You look anaemic.
MCCANN. Rheumatic.
GOLDBERG. Myopic.
MCCANN. Epileptic.
GOLDBERG. You're on the verge.
MCCANN. You're a dead duck.
GOLDBERG. But we can save you.
MCCANN. From a worse fate.
GOLDBERG. True.
MCCANN. Undeniable.
GOLDBERG. From now on, we'll be the hub of your wheel.
MCCANN. We'll renew your season ticket.
GOLDBERG. We'll take tuppence off your morning tea.
MCCANN. We'll give you a discount on all inflammable goods.
GOLDBERG. We'll watch over you.
MCCANN. Advise you.
GOLDBERG. Give you proper care and treatment.
MCCANN. Let you use the club bar.
GOLDBERG. Keep a table reserved.

MCCANN. Help you acknowledge the fast days.
GOLDBERG. Bake you cakes.
MCCANN. Help you kneel on kneeling days.
GOLDBERG. Give you a free pass.
MCCANN. Take you for constitutionals.
GOLDBERG. Give you hot tips.
MCCANN. We'll provide the skipping rope.
GOLDBERG. The vest and pants.
MCCANN. The ointment.
GOLDBERG. The hot poultice.
MCCANN. The fingerstall.
GOLDBERG. The abdomen belt.
MCCANN. The ear plugs.
GOLDBERG. The baby powder.
MCCANN. The back scratcher.
GOLDBERG. The spare tyre.
MCCANN. The stomach pump.
GOLDBERG. The oxygen tent.
MCCANN. The prayer wheel.
GOLDBERG. The plaster of Paris.
MCCANN. The crash helmet.
GOLDBERG. The crutches.
MCCANN. A day and night service.
GOLDBERG. All on the house.
MCCANN. That's it.
GOLDBERG. We'll make a man of you.
MCCANN. And a woman.
GOLDBERG. You'll be re-orientated.
MCCANN. You'll be rich.
GOLDBERG. You'll be adjusted.
MCCANN. You'll be our pride and joy.
GOLDBERG. You'll be a mensch.
MCCANN. You'll be a success.
GOLDBERG. You'll be integrated.
MCCANN. You'll give orders.
GOLDBERG. You'll make decisions.
MCCANN. You'll be a magnate.

GOLDBERG. A statesman.
MCCANN. You'll own yachts.
GOLDBERG. Animals.
MCCANN. Animals.

> GOLDBERG *looks at* MCCANN.

GOLDBERG. I said animals. (*He turns back to* STANLEY.) You'll be able to make or break, Stan. By my life. (*Silence.* STANLEY *is still.*) Well? What do you say?

> STANLEY'S *head lifts very slowly and turns in* GOLDBERG'S *direction.*

GOLDBERG. What do you think? Eh, boy?

> STANLEY *begins to clench and unclench his eyes.*

MCCANN. What's your opinion, sir? Of this prospect, sir?
GOLDBERG. Prospect. Sure. Sure it's a prospect.

> STANLEY'S *hands clutching his glasses begin to tremble.*

What's your opinion of such a prospect? Eh, Stanley?

> STANLEY *concentrates, his mouth opens, he attempts to speak, fails and emits sounds from his throat.*

STANLEY. Uh-gug . . . uh-gug . . . eeehhh-gag . . . (*On the breath.*) Caahh . . . caahh. . . .

> They watch him. He draws a long breath which shudders down his body. He concentrates.

GOLDBERG. Well, Stanny boy, what do you say, eh?

> They watch. He concentrates. His head lowers, his chin draws into his chest, he crouches.

STANLEY. Uh-gughh . . . uh-gughhh. . . .
MCCANN. What's your opinion, sir?
STANLEY. Caaahhh . . . caaahhh. . . .
MCCANN. Mr. Webber! What's your opinion?

GOLDBERG. What do you say, Stan? What do you think of the prospect?
MCCANN. What's your opinion of the prospect?

> STANLEY'S *body shudders, relaxes, his head drops, he becomes still again, stooped.* PETEY *enters from door, downstage, left.*

GOLDBERG. Still the same old Stan. Come with us. Come on, boy.
MCCANN. Come along with us.
PETEY. Where are you taking him?

They turn. Silence.

GOLDBERG. We're taking him to Monty.
PETEY. He can stay here.
GOLDBERG. Don't be silly.
PETEY. We can look after him here.
GOLDBERG. Why do you want to look after him?
PETEY. He's my guest.
GOLDBERG. He needs special treatment.
PETEY. We'll find someone.
GOLDBERG. No. Monty's the best there is. Bring him, McCann.

They help STANLEY *out of the chair.* GOLDBERG *puts the bowler hat on* STANLEY'S *head. They all three move towards the door, left.*

PETEY. Leave him alone!

They stop. GOLDBERG *studies him.*

GOLDBERG (*insidiously*). Why don't you come with us, Mr. Boles?
MCCANN. Yes, why don't you come with us?
GOLDBERG. Come with us to Monty. There's plenty of room in the car.

PETEY makes no move. They pass him and reach the

ACT III]   THE BIRTHDAY PARTY   89

> door. MCCANN *opens the door and picks up the suitcases.*

PETEY (*broken*). Stan, don't let them tell you what to do!

They exit.

> *Silence.* PETEY *stands. The front door slams. Sound of a car starting. Sound of a car going away. Silence.* PETEY *slowly goes to the table. He sits on a chair, left. He picks up the paper and opens it. The strips fall to the floor. He looks down at them.* MEG *comes past the window and enters by the back door.* PETEY *studies the front page of the paper.*

MEG (*coming downstage*). The car's gone.
PETEY. Yes.
MEG. Have they gone?
PETEY. Yes.
MEG. Won't they be in for lunch?
PETEY. No.
MEG. Oh, what a shame. (*She puts her bag on the table.*) It's hot out. (*She hangs her coat on a hook.*) What are you doing?
PETEY. Reading.
MEG. Is it good?
PETEY. All right.

> *She sits by the table.*

MEG. Where's Stan?

> *Pause.*

Is Stan down yet, Petey?
PETEY. No . . . he's. . . .
MEG. Is he still in bed?
PETEY. Yes, he's . . . still asleep.
MEG. Still? He'll be late for his breakfast.
PETEY. Let him . . . sleep.

> *Pause.*

MEG. Wasn't it a lovely party last night?
PETEY. I wasn't there.
MEG. Weren't you?
PETEY. I came in afterwards.
MEG. Oh.

Pause.

It was a lovely party. I haven't laughed so much for years. We had dancing and singing. And games. You should have been there.
PETEY. It was good, eh?

Pause.

MEG. I was the belle of the ball.
PETEY. Were you?
MEG. Oh yes. They all said I was.
PETEY. I bet you were, too.
MEG. Oh, it's true. I was.

Pause.

I know I was.

Curtain

The Room

THE ROOM was first presented at the Hampstead Theatre Club on 21st January, 1960, with the following cast:

BERT HUDD, *a man of fifty*	Howard Lang
ROSE, *a woman of sixty*	Vivien Merchant
MR. KIDD, *an old man*	Henry Woolf
MR. SANDS ⎫ *a young couple*	John Rees
MRS. SANDS ⎭	Auriol Smith
RILEY	Thomas Baptiste

THE ROOM was subsequently presented at the Royal Court Theatre on 8th March, 1960, with four changes in the cast:

BERT HUDD	Michael Brennan
MR. KIDD	John Cater
MR. SANDS	Michael Caine
MRS. SANDS	Anne Bishop

Scene: A room in a large house. A door down right. A gas-fire down left. A gas-stove and sink, up left. A window up centre. A table and chairs, centre. A rocking-chair, left centre. The foot of a double-bed protrudes from alcove, up right.

BERT *is at the table, wearing a cap, a magazine propped in front of him.* ROSE *is at the stove.*

ROSE. Here you are. This'll keep the cold out.

She places bacon and eggs on a plate, turns off the gas and takes the plate to the table.

It's very cold out, I can tell you. It's murder.

She returns to the stove and pours water from the kettle into the teapot, turns off the gas and brings the teapot to the table, pours salt and sauce on the plate and cuts two slices of bread. BERT *begins to eat.*

That's right. You eat that. You'll need it. You can feel it in here. Still, the room keeps warm. It's better than the basement, anyway.

She butters the bread.

I don't know how they live down there. It's asking for trouble. Go on. Eat it up. It'll do you good.

She goes to the sink, wipes a cup and saucer and brings them to the table.

If you want to go out you might as well have something inside you. Because you'll feel it when you get out.

She pours milk into the cup.

Just now I looked out of the window. It was enough for me. There wasn't a soul about. Can you hear the wind?

She sits in the rocking-chair.

I've never seen who it is. Who is it? Who lives down there? I'll have to ask. I mean, you might as well know, Bert. But whoever it is, it can't be too cosy.

Pause.

I think it's changed hands since I was last there. I didn't see who moved in then. I mean the first time it was taken.

Pause.

Anyway, I think they've gone now.

Pause.

But I think someone else has gone in now. I wouldn't like to live in that basement. Did you ever see the walls? They were running. This is all right for me. Go on, Bert. Have a bit more bread.

She goes to the table and cuts a slice of bread.

I'll have some cocoa on when you come back.

She goes to the window and settles the curtain.

No, this room's all right for me. I mean, you know where you are. When it's cold, for instance.

She goes to the table.

What about the rasher? Was it all right? It was a good one, I know, but not as good as the last lot I got in. It's the weather.

She goes to the rocking-chair, and sits.

Anyway, I haven't been out. I haven't been so well. I didn't feel up to it. Still, I'm much better today. I don't know about you though. I don't know whether you ought to go out. I mean, you shouldn't, straight after you've been laid up. Still. Don't worry, Bert. You go. You won't be long.

She rocks.

It's good you were up here, I can tell you. It's good you weren't down there, in the basement. That's no joke. Oh, I've left the tea. I've left the tea standing.

She goes to the table and pours tea into the cup.

No, it's not bad. Nice weak tea. Lovely weak tea. Here you are. Drink it down. I'll wait for mine. Anyway, I'll have it a bit stronger.

She takes a plate to the sink and leaves it.

Those walls would have finished you off. I don't know who lives down there now. Whoever it is, they're taking a big chance. Maybe they're foreigners.

She goes to the rocking-chair and sits.

I'd have pulled you through.

Pause.

There isn't room for two down there, anyway. I think there was one first, before he moved out. Maybe they've got two now.

She rocks.

If they ever ask you, Bert, I'm quite happy where I am. We're quiet, we're all right. You're happy up here. It's not far up either, when you come in from outside. And we're not bothered. And nobody bothers us.

Pause.

I don't know why you have to go out. Couldn't you run it down tomorrow? I could put the fire in later. You could sit by the fire. That's what you like, Bert, of an evening. It'll be dark in a minute as well, soon.

She rocks.

It gets dark now.

She rises and pours out tea at the table.

I made plenty. Go on.

She sits at table.

You looked out today? It's got ice on the roads. Oh, I know you can drive. I'm not saying you can't drive. I mentioned to Mr. Kidd this morning that you'd be doing a run today. I told him you hadn't been too grand, but I said, still, he's a marvellous driver. I wouldn't mind what time, where, nothing, Bert. You know how to drive. I told him.

She wraps her cardigan about her.

But it's cold. It's really cold today, chilly. I'll have you some nice cocoa on for when you get back.

She rises, goes to the window, and looks out.

It's quiet. Be coming on for dark. There's no one about.

She stands, looking.

Wait a minute.

Pause.

I wonder who that is.

Pause.

No. I thought I saw someone.

Pause.

No.

She drops the curtain.

You know what though? It looks a bit better. It's not so windy. You'd better put on your thick jersey.

She goes to the rocking-chair, sits and rocks.

This is a good room. You've got a chance in a place like this. I look after you, don't I, Bert? Like when they offered us the basement here I said no straight off. I knew that'd be no good. The ceiling right on top of you. No, you've got a window here, you can move yourself, you can come home at night, if you have to go out, you can do your job, you can come home, you're all right. And I'm here. You stand a chance.

Pause.

I wonder who has got it now. I've never seen them, or heard of them. But I think someone's down there. Whoever's got it can keep it. That looked a good rasher, Bert. I'll have a cup of tea later. I like mine a bit stronger. You like yours weak.

A knock at the door. She stands.

Who is it?

Pause.

Hallo!

Knock repeated.

Come in then.

Knock repeated.

Who is it?

Pause. The door opens and MR. KIDD *comes in.*

MR. KIDD. I knocked.
ROSE. I heard you.
MR. KIDD. Eh?
ROSE. We heard you.
MR. KIDD. Hallo, Mr. Hudd, how are you, all right? I've been looking at the pipes.
ROSE. Are they all right?

MR. KIDD. Eh?
ROSE. Sit down, Mr. Kidd.
MR. KIDD. No, that's all right. I just popped in, like, to see how things were going. Well, it's cosy in here, isn't it?
ROSE. Oh, thank you, Mr. Kidd.
MR. KIDD. You going out today, Mr. Hudd? I went out. I came straight in again. Only to the corner, of course.
ROSE. Not many people about today, Mr. Kidd.
MR. KIDD. So I thought to myself, I'd better have a look at those pipes. In the circumstances. I only went to the corner, for a few necessary items. It's likely to snow. Very likely, in my opinion.
ROSE. Why don't you sit down, Mr. Kidd?
MR. KIDD. No, no, that's all right.
ROSE. Well, it's a shame you have to go out in this weather, Mr. Kidd. Don't you have a help?
MR. KIDD. Eh?
ROSE. I thought you had a woman to help.
MR. KIDD. I haven't got any woman.
ROSE. I thought you had one when we first came.
MR. KIDD. No women here.
ROSE. Maybe I was thinking of somewhere else.
MR. KIDD. Plenty of women round the corner. Not here though. Oh no. Eh, have I seen that before?
ROSE. What?
MR. KIDD. That.
ROSE. I don't know. Have you?
MR. KIDD. I seem to have some remembrance.
ROSE. It's just an old rocking-chair.
MR. KIDD. Was it here when you came?
ROSE. No, I brought it myself.
MR. KIDD. I could swear blind I've seen that before.
ROSE. Perhaps you have.
MR. KIDD. What?
ROSE. I say, perhaps you have.
MR. KIDD. Yes, maybe I have.
ROSE. Take a seat, Mr. Kidd.

MR. KIDD. I wouldn't take an oath on it though.

BERT *yawns and stretches, and continues looking at his magazine.*

No, I won't sit down, with Mr. Hudd just having a bit of a rest after his tea. I've got to go and get mine going in a minute. You're going out then, Mr. Hudd? I was just looking at your van. She's a very nice little van, that. I notice you wrap her up well for the cold. I don't blame you. Yes, I was hearing you go off, when was it, the other morning, yes. Very smooth. I can tell a good gear-change.

ROSE. I thought your bedroom was at the back, Mr. Kidd.
MR. KIDD. My bedroom?
ROSE. Wasn't it at the back? Not that I ever knew.
MR. KIDD. I wasn't in my bedroom.
ROSE. Oh, well.
MR. KIDD. I was up and about.
ROSE. I don't get up early in this weather. I can take my time. I take my time.

Pause.

MR. KIDD. This was my bedroom.
ROSE. This? When?
MR. KIDD. When I lived here.
ROSE. I didn't know that.
MR. KIDD. I will sit down for a few ticks. (*He sits in the armchair.*)
ROSE. Well, I never knew that.
MR. KIDD. Was this chair here when you came?
ROSE. Yes.
MR. KIDD. I can't recollect this one.

Pause.

ROSE. When was that then?
MR. KIDD. Eh?
ROSE. When was this your bedroom?
MR. KIDD. A good while back.

Pause.

ROSE. I was telling Bert I was telling you how he could drive.
MR. KIDD. Mr. Hudd? Oh, Mr. Hudd can drive all right. I've seen him bowl down the road all right. Oh yes.
ROSE. Well, Mr. Kidd, I must say this is a very nice room. It's a very comfortable room.
MR. KIDD. Best room in the house.
ROSE. It must get a bit damp downstairs.
MR. KIDD. Not as bad as upstairs.
ROSE. What about downstairs?
MR. KIDD. Eh?
ROSE. What about downstairs?
MR. KIDD. What about it?
ROSE. Must get a bit damp.
MR. KIDD. A bit. Not as bad as upstairs though.
ROSE. Why's that?
MR. KIDD. The rain comes in.

Pause.

ROSE. Anyone live up there?
MR. KIDD. Up there? There was. Gone now.
ROSE. How many floors you got in this house?
MR. KIDD. Floors. (*He laughs.*) Ah, we had a good few of them in the old days.
ROSE. How many have you got now?
MR. KIDD. Well, to tell you the truth, I don't count them now.
ROSE. Oh.
MR. KIDD. No, not now.
ROSE. It must be a bit of a job.
MR. KIDD. Oh, I used to count them, once. Never got tired of it. I used to keep a tack on everything in this house. I had a lot to keep my eye on, then. I was able for it too. That was when my sister was alive. But I lost track a bit, after she died. She's been dead some time now, my sister. It was a good house then. She was a capable woman.

Yes. Fine size of a woman too. I think she took after my mum. Yes, I think she took after my old mum, from what I can recollect. I think my mum was a Jewess. Yes, I wouldn't be surprised to learn that she was a Jewess. She didn't have many babies.

ROSE. What about your sister, Mr. Kidd?

MR. KIDD. What about her?

ROSE. Did she have any babies?

MR. KIDD. Yes, she had a resemblance to my old mum, I think. Taller, of course.

ROSE. When did she die then, your sister?

MR. KIDD. Yes, that's right, it was after she died that I must have stopped counting. She used to keep things in very good trim. And I gave her a helping hand. She was very grateful, right until her last. She always used to tell me how much she appreciated all the—little things—that I used to do for her. Then she copped it. I was her senior. Yes, I was her senior. She had a lovely boudoir. A beautiful boudoir.

ROSE. What did she die of?

MR. KIDD. Who?

ROSE. Your sister.

Pause.

MR. KIDD. I've made ends meet.

Pause.

ROSE. You full at the moment, Mr. Kidd?

MR. KIDD. Packed out.

ROSE. All sorts, I suppose?

MR. KIDD. Oh yes, I make ends meet.

ROSE. We do, too, don't we, Bert?

Pause.

Where's your bedroom now then, Mr. Kidd?

MR. KIDD. Me? I can take my pick. (*Rising.*) You'll be going out soon then, Mr. Hudd? Well, be careful how you go. Those roads'll be no joke. Still, you know how to manipulate your van all right, don't you? Where you going? Far? Be long?

ROSE. He won't be long.

MR. KIDD. No, of course not. Shouldn't take him long.

ROSE. No.

MR. KIDD. Well then, I'll pop off. Have a good run, Mr. Hudd. Mind how you go. It'll be dark soon too. But not for a good while yet. Arivederci.

He exits.

ROSE. I don't believe he had a sister, ever.

She takes the plate and cup to the sink. BERT *pushes his chair back and rises.*

All right. Wait a minute. Where's your jersey?

She brings the jersey from the bed.

Here you are. Take your coat off. Get into it.

She helps him into his jersey.

Right. Where's your muffler?

She brings a muffler from the bed.

Here you are. Wrap it round. That's it. Don't go too fast, Bert, will you? I'll have some cocoa on when you get back. You won't be long. Wait a minute. Where's your overcoat? You'd better put on your overcoat.

He fixes his muffler, goes to the door and exits. She stands, watching the door, then turns slowly to the table, picks up the magazine, and puts it down. She stands and listens, goes to the fire, bends, lights the fire and warms her hands. She stands and looks about the room. She looks at the window and listens, goes quickly to the window, stops and straightens the curtain. She comes to the centre of the room, and looks towards the door. She goes to the bed, puts on a shawl, goes to the sink, takes a bin from under the sink, goes to the door and opens it.

ROSE. Oh!

MR. *and* MRS. SANDS *are disclosed on the landing.*

MRS. SANDS. So sorry. We didn't mean to be standing here, like. Didn't mean to give you a fright. We've just come up the stairs.

ROSE. That's all right.

MRS. SANDS. This is Mr. Sands. I'm Mrs. Sands.

ROSE. How do you do?

MR. SANDS *grunts acknowledgement.*

MRS. SANDS. We were just going up the stairs. But you can't see a thing in this place. Can you, Toddy?

MR. SANDS. Not a thing.

ROSE. What were you looking for?

MRS. SANDS. The man who runs the house.

MR. SANDS. The landlord. We're trying to get hold of the landlord.

MRS. SANDS. What's his name, Toddy?

ROSE. His name's Mr. Kidd.

MRS. SANDS. Kidd? Was that the name, Toddy?

MR. SANDS. Kidd? No, that's not it.

ROSE. Mr. Kidd. That's his name.

MR. SANDS. Well, that's not the bloke we're looking for.

ROSE. Well, you must be looking for someone else.

Pause.

MR. SANDS. I suppose we must be.

ROSE. You look cold.

MRS. SANDS. It's murder out. Have you been out?

ROSE. No.

MRS. SANDS. We've not long come in.

ROSE. Well, come inside, if you like, and have a warm.

They come into the centre of the room.

(*Bringing the chair from the table to the fire*). Sit down here. You can get a good warm

MRS. SANDS. Thanks. (*She sits.*)

ROSE. Come over by the fire, Mr. Sands.

MR. SANDS. No, it's all right. I'll just stretch my legs.

MRS. SANDS. Why? You haven't been sitting down.

MR. SANDS. What about it?

MRS. SANDS. Well, why don't you sit down?

MR. SANDS. Why should I?

MRS. SANDS. You must be cold.

MR. SANDS. I'm not.

MRS. SANDS. You must be. Bring over a chair and sit down.

MR. SANDS. I'm all right standing up, thanks.

MRS. SANDS. You don't look one thing or the other standing up.

MR. SANDS. I'm quite all right, Clarissa.

ROSE. Clarissa? What a pretty name.

MRS. SANDS. Yes, it is nice, isn't it? My father and mother gave it to me.

Pause.

You know, this is a room you can sit down and feel cosy in.

MR. SANDS (*looking at the room*). It's a fair size, all right.

MRS. SANDS. Why don't you sit down, Mrs.—

ROSE. Hudd. No thanks.

MR. SANDS. What did you say?

ROSE. When?

MR. SANDS. What did you say the name was?

ROSE. Hudd.

MR. SANDS. That's it. You're the wife of the bloke you mentioned then?

MRS. SANDS. No, she isn't. That was Mr. Kidd.

MR. SANDS. Was it? I thought it was Hudd.

MRS. SANDS. No, it was Kidd. Wasn't it, Mrs. Hudd?

ROSE. That's right. The landlord.

MRS. SANDS. No, not the landlord. The other man.

ROSE. Well, that's his name. He's the landlord.
MR. SANDS. Who?
ROSE. Mr. Kidd.

Pause.

MR. SANDS. Is he?
MRS. SANDS. Maybe there are two landlords.

Pause.

MR. SANDS. That'll be the day.
MRS. SANDS. What did you say?
MR. SANDS. I said that'll be the day.

Pause.

ROSE. What's it like out?
MRS. SANDS. It's very dark out.
MR. SANDS. No darker than in.
MRS. SANDS. He's right there.
MR. SANDS. It's darker in than out, for my money.
MRS. SANDS. There's not much light in this place, is there, Mrs. Hudd? Do you know, this is the first bit of light we've seen since we came in?
MR. SANDS. The first crack.
ROSE. I never go out at night. We stay in.
MRS. SANDS. Now I come to think of it, I saw a star.
MR. SANDS. You saw what?
MRS. SANDS. Well, I think I did.
MR. SANDS. You think you saw what?
MRS. SANDS. A star.
MR. SANDS. Where?
MRS. SANDS. In the sky.
MR. SANDS. When?
MRS. SANDS. As we were coming along.
MR. SANDS. Go home.
MRS. SANDS. What do you mean?
MR. SANDS. You didn't see a star.
MRS. SANDS. Why not?

MR. SANDS. Because I'm telling you. I'm telling you you didn't see a star.

Pause.

ROSE. I hope it's not too dark out. I hope it's not too icy. My husband's in his van. He doesn't drive slow either. He never drives slow.

MR. SANDS (*guffawing*). Well, he's taking a big chance tonight then.

ROSE. What?

MR. SANDS. No—I mean, it'd be a bit dodgy driving tonight.

ROSE. He's a very good driver.

Pause.

How long have you been here?

MRS. SANDS. I don't know. How long have we been here, Toddy?

MR. SANDS. About half an hour.

MRS. SANDS. Longer than that, much longer.

MR. SANDS. About thirty-five minutes.

ROSE. Well, I think you'll find Mr. Kidd about somewhere. He's not long gone to make his tea.

MR. SANDS. He lives here, does he?

ROSE. Of course he lives here.

MR. SANDS. And you say he's the landlord, is he?

ROSE. Of course he is.

MR. SANDS. Well, say I wanted to get hold of him, where would I find him?

ROSE. Well—I'm not sure.

MR. SANDS. He lives here, does he?

ROSE. Yes, but I don't know—

MR. SANDS. You don't know exactly where he hangs out?

ROSE. No, not exactly.

MR. SANDS. But he does live here, doesn't he?

Pause.

MRS. SANDS. This is a very big house, Toddy.

MR. SANDS. Yes, I know it is. But Mrs. Hudd seems to know Mr. Kidd very well.
ROSE. No, I wouldn't say that. As a matter of fact, I don't know him at all. We're very quiet. We keep ourselves to ourselves. I never interfere. I mean, why should I? We've got our room. We don't bother anyone else. That's the way it should be.
MRS. SANDS. It's a nice house, isn't it? Roomy.
ROSE. I don't know about the house. We're all right, but I wouldn't mind betting there's a lot wrong with this house. (*She sits in the rocking-chair.*) I think there's a lot of damp.
MRS. SANDS. Yes, I felt a bit of damp when we were in the basement just now.
ROSE. You were in the basement?
MRS. SANDS. Yes, we went down there when we came in.
ROSE. Why?
MRS. SANDS. We were looking for the landlord.
ROSE. What was it like down there?
MR. SANDS. Couldn't see a thing.
ROSE. Why not?
MR. SANDS. There wasn't any light.
ROSE. But what was—you said it was damp?
MRS. SANDS. I felt a bit, didn't you, Tod?
MR. SANDS. Why? Haven't you ever been down there, Mrs. Hudd?
ROSE. Oh yes, once, a long time ago.
MR. SANDS. Well, you know what it's like then, don't you?
ROSE. It was a long time ago.
MR. SANDS. You haven't been here all that long, have you?
ROSE. I was just wondering whether anyone was living down there now.
MRS. SANDS. Yes. A man.
ROSE. A man?
MRS. SANDS. Yes.
ROSE. One man?
MR. SANDS. Yes, there was a bloke down there, all right.

He perches on the table.

MRS. SANDS. You're sitting down!
MR. SANDS (*jumping up*). Who is?
MRS. SANDS. You were.
MR. SANDS. Don't be silly. I perched.
MRS. SANDS. I saw you sit down.
MR. SANDS. You did not see me sit down because I did not sit bloody well down. I perched!
MRS. SANDS. Do you think I can't perceive when someone's sitting down?
MR. SANDS. Perceive! That's all you do. Perceive.
MRS. SANDS. You could do with a bit more of that instead of all that tripe you get up to.
MR. SANDS. You don't mind some of that tripe!
MRS. SANDS. You take after your uncle, that's who you take after!
MR. SANDS. And who do you take after?
MRS. SANDS (*rising*). I didn't bring you into the world.
MR. SANDS. You didn't what?
MRS. SANDS. I said, I didn't bring you into the world.
MR. SANDS. Well, who did then? That's what I want to know. Who did? Who did bring me into the world?

She sits, muttering. He stands, muttering.

ROSE. You say you saw a man downstairs, in the basement?
MRS. SANDS. Yes, Mrs. Hudd, you see, the thing is, Mrs. Hudd, we'd heard they'd got a room to let here, so we thought we'd come along and have a look. Because we're looking for a place, you see, somewhere quiet, and we knew this district was quiet, and we passed the house a few months ago and we thought it looked very nice, but we thought we'd call of an evening, to catch the landlord, so we came along this evening. Well, when we got here we walked in the front door and it was very dark in the hall and there wasn't anyone about. So we went down to the basement. Well, we got down there only due to Toddy

having such good eyesight really. Between you and me, I didn't like the look of it much, I mean the feel, we couldn't make much out, it smelt damp to me. Anyway, we went through a kind of partition, then there was another partition, and we couldn't see where we were going, well, it seemed to me it got darker the more we went, the further we went in, I thought we must have come to the wrong house. So I stopped. And Toddy stopped. And then this voice said, this voice came—it said—well, it gave me a bit of a fright, I don't know about Tod, but someone asked if he could do anything for us. So Tod said we were looking for the landlord and this man said the landlord would be upstairs. Then Tod asked was there a room vacant. And this man, this voice really, I think he was behind the partition, said yes there was a room vacant. He was very polite, I thought, but we never saw him, I don't know why they never put a light on. Anyway, we got out then and we came up and we went to the top of the house. I don't know whether it was the top. There was a door locked on the stairs, so there might have been another floor, but we didn't see anyone, and it was dark, and we were just coming down again when you opened your door.

ROSE. You said you were going up.
MRS. SANDS. What?
ROSE. You said you were going up before.
MRS. SANDS. No, we were coming down.
ROSE. You didn't say that before.
MRS. SANDS. We'd been up.
MR. SANDS. We'd been up. We were coming down.

Pause.

ROSE. This man, what was he like, was he old?
MRS. SANDS. We didn't see him.
ROSE. Was he old?

Pause.

MR. SANDS. Well, we'd better try to get hold of this landlord, if he's about.
ROSE. You won't find any rooms vacant in this house.
MR. SANDS. Why not?
ROSE. Mr. Kidd told me. He told me.
MR. SANDS. Mr. Kidd?
ROSE. He told me he was full up.
MR. SANDS. The man in the basement said there was one. One room. Number seven he said.

Pause.

ROSE. That's this room.
MR. SANDS. We'd better go and get hold of the landlord.
MRS. SANDS (*rising*). Well, thank you for the warm-up, Mrs. Hudd. I feel better now.
ROSE. This room is occupied.
MR. SANDS. Come on.
MRS. SANDS. Goodnight, Mrs. Hudd. I hope your husband won't be too long. Must be lonely for you, being all alone here.
MR. SANDS. Come on.

They go out. ROSE *watches the door close, starts towards it, and stops. She takes the chair back to the table, picks up the magazine, looks at it, and puts it down. She goes to the rocking-chair, sits, rocks, stops, and sits still. There is a sharp knock at the door, which opens. Enter* MR. KIDD.

MR. KIDD. I came straight in.
ROSE (*rising*). Mr. Kidd! I was just going to find you. I've got to speak to you.
MR. KIDD. Look here, Mrs. Hudd, I've got to speak to you. I came up specially.
ROSE. There were two people in here just now. They said this room was going vacant. What were they talking about?

MR. KIDD. As soon as I heard the van go I got ready to come and see you. I'm knocked out.

ROSE. What was it all about? Did you see those people? How can this room be going? It's occupied. Did they get hold of you, Mr. Kidd?

MR. KIDD. Get hold of me? Who?

ROSE. I told you. Two people. They were looking for the landlord.

MR. KIDD. I'm just telling you. I've been getting ready to come and see you, as soon as I heard the van go.

ROSE. Well then, who were they?

MR. KIDD. That's why I came up before. But he hadn't gone yet. I've been waiting for him to go the whole week-end.

ROSE. Mr. Kidd, what did they mean about this room?

MR. KIDD. What room?

ROSE. Is this room vacant?

MR. KIDD. Vacant?

ROSE. They were looking for the landlord.

MR. KIDD. Who were?

ROSE. Listen, Mr. Kidd, you are the landlord, aren't you? There isn't any other landlord?

MR. KIDD. What? What's that got to do with it? I don't know what you're talking about. I've got to tell you, that's all. I've got to tell you. I've had a terrible week-end. You'll have to see him. I can't take it any more. You've got to see him.

Pause.

ROSE. Who?

MR. KIDD. The man. He's been waiting to see you. He wants to see you. I can't get rid of him. I'm not a young man, Mrs. Hudd, that's apparent. It's apparent. You've got to see him.

ROSE. See who?

MR. KIDD. The man. He's downstairs now. He's been there the whole week-end. He said that when Mr. Hudd went out I was to tell him. That's why I came up before. But he hadn't gone yet. So I told him. I said he hasn't gone yet. I said, well when he goes, I said, you can go up, go up, have done with it. No, he says, you must ask her if she'll see me. So I came up again, to ask you if you'll see him.

ROSE. Who is he?

MR. KIDD. How do I know who he is? All I know is he won't say a word, he won't indulge in any conversation, just— has he gone? that and nothing else. He wouldn't even play a game of chess. All right, I said, the other night, while we're waiting I'll play you a game of chess. You play chess, don't you? I tell you, Mrs. Hudd, I don't know if he even heard what I was saying. He just lies there. It's not good for me. He just lies there, that's all, waiting.

ROSE. He lies there, in the basement?

MR. KIDD. Shall I tell him it's all right, Mrs. Hudd?

ROSE. But it's damp down there.

MR. KIDD. Shall I tell him it's all right?

ROSE. That what's all right?

MR. KIDD. That you'll see him.

ROSE. See him? I beg your pardon, Mr. Kidd. I don't know him. Why should I see him?

MR. KIDD. You won't see him?

ROSE. Do you expect me to see someone I don't know? With my husband not here too?

MR. KIDD. But he knows you, Mrs. Hudd, he knows you.

ROSE. How could he, Mr. Kidd, when I don't know him?

MR. KIDD. You must know him.

ROSE. But I don't know anybody. We're quiet here. We've just moved into this district.

MR. KIDD. But he doesn't come from this district. Perhaps you knew him in another district.

ROSE. Mr. Kidd, do you think I go around knowing men in one district after another? What do you think I am?

MR. KIDD. I don't know what I think.

He sits.

I think I'm going off my squiff.

ROSE. You need rest. An old man like you. What you need is rest.

MR. KIDD. He hasn't given me any rest. Just lying there. In the black dark. Hour after hour. Why don't you leave me be, both of you? Mrs. Hudd, have a bit of pity. Please see him. Why don't you see him?

ROSE. I don't know him.

MR. KIDD. You can never tell. You might know him.

ROSE. I don't know him.

MR. KIDD (*rising*). I don't know what'll happen if you don't see him.

ROSE. I've told you I don't know this man!

MR. KIDD. I know what he'll do. I know what he'll do. If you don't see him now, there'll be nothing else for it, he'll come up on his own bat, when your husband's here, that's what he'll do. He'll come up when Mr. Hudd's here, when your husband's here.

ROSE. He'd never do that.

MR. KIDD. He would do that. That's exactly what he'll do. You don't think he's going to go away without seeing you, after he's come all this way, do you? You don't think that, do you?

ROSE. All this way?

MR. KIDD. You don't think he's going to do that, do you?

Pause.

ROSE. He wouldn't do that.

MR. KIDD. Oh yes. I know it.

Pause.

ROSE. What's the time?

MR. KIDD. I don't know.

Pause.

ROSE. Fetch him. Quick. Quick!

> MR. KIDD *goes out. She sits in the rocking-chair. After a few moments the door opens. Enter a blind Negro. He closes the door behind him, walks further, and feels with a stick till he reaches the armchair. He stops.*

RILEY. Mrs. Hudd?
ROSE. You just touched a chair. Why don't you sit in it?

He sits.

RILEY. Thank you.
ROSE. Don't thank me for anything. I don't want you up here. I don't know who you are. And the sooner you get out the better.

Pause.

(*Rising.*) Well, come on. Enough's enough. You can take a liberty too far, you know. What do you want? You force your way up here. You disturb my evening. You come in and sit down here. What do you want?

He looks about the room.

What are you looking at? You're blind, aren't you? So what are you looking at? What do you think you've got here, a little girl? I can keep up with you. I'm one ahead of people like you. Tell me what you want and get out.
RILEY. My name is Riley.
ROSE. I don't care if it's—What? That's not your name. That's not your name. You've got a grown-up woman in this room, do you hear? Or are you deaf too? You're not deaf too, are you? You're all deaf and dumb and blind, the lot of you. A bunch of cripples.

Pause.

RILEY. This is a large room.
ROSE. Never mind about the room. What do you know about

this room? You know nothing about it. And you won't be staying in it long either. My luck. I get these creeps come in, smelling up my room. What do you want?

RILEY. I want to see you.

ROSE. Well you can't see me, can you? You're a blind man. An old, poor blind man. Aren't you? Can't see a dickey-bird.

Pause.

They say I know you. That's an insult, for a start. Because I can tell you, I wouldn't know you to spit on, not from a mile off.

Pause.

Oh, these customers. They come in here and stink the place out. After a handout. I know all about it. And as for you saying you know me, what liberty is that? Telling my landlord too. Upsetting my landlord. What do you think you're up to? We're settled down here, cosy, quiet, and our landlord thinks the world of us, we're his favourite tenants, and you come in and drive him up the wall, and drag my name into it! What did you mean by dragging my name into it, and my husband's name? How did you know what our name was?

Pause.

You've led him a dance, have you, this week-end? You've got him going, have you? A poor, weak old man, who lets a respectable house. Finished. Done for. You push your way in and shove him about. And you drag my name into it.

Pause.

Come on, then. You say you wanted to see me. Well, I'm here. Spit it out or out you go. What do you want?

RILEY. I have a message for you.

ROSE. You've got what? How could you have a message for

me, Mister Riley, when I don't know you and nobody knows I'm here and I don't know anybody anyway. You think I'm an easy touch, don't you? Well, why don't you give it up as a bad job? Get off out of it. I've had enough of this. You're not only a nut, you're a blind nut and you can get out the way you came.

Pause.

What message? Who have you got a message from? Who?
RILEY. Your father wants you to come home.

Pause.

ROSE. Home?
RILEY. Yes.
ROSE. Home? Go now. Come on. It's late. It's late.
RILEY. To come home.
ROSE. Stop it. I can't take it. What do you want? What do you want?
RILEY. Come home, Sal.

Pause.

ROSE. What did you call me?
RILEY. Come home, Sal.
ROSE. Don't call me that.
RILEY. Come, now.
ROSE. Don't call me that.
RILEY. So now you're here.
ROSE. Not Sal.
RILEY. Now I touch you.
ROSE. Don't touch me.
RILEY. Sal.
ROSE. I can't.
RILEY. I want you to come home.
ROSE. No.
RILEY. With me.
ROSE. I can't.
RILEY. I waited to see you.

ROSE. Yes.
RILEY. Now I see you.
ROSE. Yes.
RILEY. Sal.
ROSE. Not that.
RILEY. So, now.

Pause.

So, now.
ROSE. I've been here.
RILEY. Yes.
ROSE. Long.
RILEY. Yes.
ROSE. The day is a hump. I never go out.
RILEY. No.
ROSE. I've been here.
RILEY. Come home now, Sal.

She touches his eyes, the back of his head and his temples with her hands. Enter BERT.
He stops at the door, then goes to the window and draws the curtains. It is dark. He comes to the centre of the room and regards the woman.

BERT. I got back all right.
ROSE (*going towards him*). Yes.
BERT. I got back all right.

Pause.

ROSE. Is it late?
BERT. I had a good bowl down there.

Pause.

I drove her down, hard. They got it dark out.
ROSE. Yes.
BERT. Then I drove her back, hard. They got it very icy out.
ROSE. Yes.
BERT. But I drove her.

Pause.

I sped her.

Pause.

I caned her along. She was good. Then I got back. I could see the road all right. There was no cars. One there was. He wouldn't move. I bumped him. I got my road. I had all my way. There again and back. They shoved out of it. I kept on the straight. There was no mixing it. Not with her. She was good. She went with me. She don't mix it with me. I use my hand. Like that. I get hold of her. I go where I go. She took me there. She brought me back.

Pause.

I got back all right.

He takes the chair from the table and sits to the left of the NEGRO'S *chair, close to it. He regards the* NEGRO *for some moments. Then with his foot he lifts the armchair up. The* NEGRO *falls on to the floor. He rises slowly.*

RILEY. Mr. Hudd, your wife—
BERT. Lice!

He strikes the NEGRO, *knocking him down, and then kicks his head against the gas-stove several times. The* NEGRO *lies still.* BERT *walks away.*
Silence.
ROSE *stands clutching her eyes.*

ROSE. Can't see. I can't see. I can't see.

Blackout

Curtain